A Famine for the Word of God

Are You Being Fully Nourished?

Lamar Mauldin, Sr.

TEACH Services, Inc.
PUBLISHING
www.TEACHServices.com • (800) 367-1844

World rights reserved. This book or any portion thereof may not be copied or reproduced in any form or manner whatever, except as provided by law, without the written permission of the publisher, except by a reviewer who may quote brief passages in a review.

The author assumes full responsibility for the accuracy of all facts and quotations as cited in this book. The opinions expressed in this book are the author's personal views and interpretations, and do not necessarily reflect those of the publisher.

This book is provided with the understanding that the publisher is not engaged in giving spiritual, legal, medical, or other professional advice. If authoritative advice is needed, the reader should seek the counsel of a competent professional.

Copyright © 2020 Lamar Mauldin, Sr.
Copyright © 2020 TEACH Services, Inc.
ISBN-13: 978-1-4796-0951-2 (Paperback)
ISBN-13: 978-1-4796-0952-9 (ePub)
Library of Congress Control Number: 2018913678

King James Version (KJV)
Public Domain

New International Version (NIV)
Holy Bible, New International Version®, NIV® Copyright © 1973, 1978, 1984, 2011 by Biblica, Inc.® Used by permission. All rights reserved worldwide.

New International Reader's Version (NIRV)
Copyright © 1995, 1996, 1998, 2014 by Biblica, Inc.®. Used by permission. All rights reserved worldwide.

Queen James Version (QJV)
© 2012 by QueenJamesBible.com
All rights reserved. No part of this book may be reproduced or transmitted in any form or by any means, electronic or mechanical, including photocopy, recording, or any information storage or retrieval system, without prior written permission from the publisher, except by a reviewer, who may quote short excerpts in a review.
First Edition.

New King James Version (NKJV)
Scripture taken from the New King James Version®. Copyright © 1982 by Thomas Nelson. Used by permission. All rights reserved.

Published by

www.TEACHServices.com • (800) 367-1844

Table of Contents

Preface . . . . *vii*
Introduction . . . . *x*

1. **The Conspiracy** **13**
   Brooke Foss Westcott 19
   Fenton John Anthony Hort 21

2. **Spurious Bible Versions** **24**

3. **Unmasking the NKJV and the NASB** **29**
   The NASB Scandal 29
   The NKJV Debacle 31

4. **Precept Upon Precept Line Upon Line** **38**
   Subtle Deception 42
   Missing Verses 43
   Changes and Deletions 54

5.	In Spite of, Not Because of	67
6.	Is Jesus The Christ?	74
7.	The Mark of the Beast	91
8.	**The New (age) King James Versions**	117
	Spiritualism	119
	Ecumenism	125
9.	**Ellen White's Use of Modern Bible Versions**	132
	Divine Preservation	134
	A Perfect Chain	136
	Vindication of the AV and the Prophet	138
10.	The Destruction of the Sanctuary	146
11.	The Conclusion of the Matter	161

Those who do not now appreciate, study, and dearly prize the Word of God, spoken by His servants, will have cause to mourn bitterly hereafter. I saw that the Lord in judgment will, at the close of time, walk through the earth; the fearful plagues will begin to fall. Then those who have despised God's Word, those who have lightly esteemed it, shall wander from sea to sea, and from the north even to the east; they shall run to and fro to seek the Word of the Lord and shall not find it. A famine is in the land for hearing the Word.
(White, *Manuscript Releases*, Vol. 1, 1857)

Preface

"Ye shall not add unto the word which I command you,
neither shall ye diminish ought from it, that ye may
keep the commandments of the LORD your God
which I command you" (Deut. 4:2, KJV).

This book is not intended to be a scholarly work addressing the accuracy or inaccuracy of languages and manuscripts. Although some of that is done, the focus of this writing is to look at the spiritual ramifications and significance of changing words, phrases, and verses in the Bible, and to expose thereby the agenda of our common enemy, the devil, and his desire to unsettle our faith in God's Word.

We are told in the Authorized Version, the King James Bible, in 2 Corinthians 2:11, "Lest Satan should get an advantage of us: for we are not ignorant of his devices." One admonition we can draw from this verse and the context it is set in is that God does not want us to be ignorant of the devil's devices. One such device is the creation of modern Bibles that change certain words that can and often does, cause a shift in the meaning of a verse, which can alter the contextual meaning and even doctrine.

For example, the verse used above, 2 Corinthians 2:11, many of the modern versions replace the adjective 'ignorant,' which means a lack of knowledge or understanding and experience, with another adjective having a lesser encompassing meaning. In the case of the New International Version the word 'unaware,' although similar in meaning, can have a very different connotation, and replaces the word 'ignorant.' This subtle change in wording not only allows for copyright protections for producers of modern versions for financial gain but also allows Satan to distort the verse for his purposes. Because modern version producers hold to the idea that translation of the Bible is never a completed work, because languages change with the passage of time, Satan will use those translations to replace further words drawing the Bible student even further away from the meaning originally intended by God.

In the same verse, the noun "devices," which means, in this case, a way of achieving something dishonestly, is replaced with the adjective 'schemes.' Although these words are similar in meaning a program of changing words opens the door for future changes that can and will take our understanding in a direction that God would not have them go.

The King James Bible in 1 Peter 5:8 also admonishes us to "Be sober, be vigilant; because your adversary the devil, as a roaring lion, walketh about, seeking whom he may devour." Modern versions, the NIV in this case, replace the words *'sober'* and *'vigilant'* with *'self-controlled'* and *'alert.'* Of course, the casual reader will most likely overlook this subtle change. A closer examination reveals that these changes in wording can easily convey an entirely different spiritual meaning of the verse. If the reader were sober, vigilant, and alert, especially to guard against danger, difficulties, or errors, he would understand that even the drunken man believes he is in control of himself, and to be alert is one component of what it means to be vigilant.

God wants us to be on guard always against the subtle attacks of the devil. The words *self-controlled* and *alert* fall short of conveying the true import of 1 Peter 5:8. By accepting the subtle changes in the modern versions, we do the opposite of what the verse requires.

Not everyone involved with the production of modern versions is knowingly working to deceive. However, when the Bible is viewed as merchandise, many lose sight of God's intent for His word and end up unintentionally working for the cause of Satan. It is the prayerful hope and intent of this author to use enough examples of distorted modern version texts to prove a program of intent to deceive and cause many to lose faith in the Scriptures.

Introduction

Human minds vary. The minds of different education and thought receive different impressions of the same words, and it is difficult for one mind to give to one of a different temperament, education, and habits of thought by language exactly the same idea as that which is clear and distinct in his own mind. Yet to honest men, right-minded men, he can be so simple and plain as to convey his meaning for all practical purposes. If the man he communicates with is not honest and will not want to see and understand the truth, he will turn his words and language in everything to suit his own purposes. He will misconstrue his words, play upon his imagination, wrest them from their true meaning, and then entrench himself in unbelief, claiming that the sentiments are all wrong.

This is the way my writings are treated by those who wish to misunderstand and pervert them. They turn the truth of God into a lie. In the very same way that they treat the writings in my published articles and in my books, so do skeptics and infidels treat the Bible. **They read it according to their desire to pervert, to misapply, to willfully wrest the utterances from their true meaning**. They declare that the Bible can prove anything and everything, that every sect proves their doctrines right, and that the most diverse doctrines are proved from the Bible.

The writers of the Bible had to express their ideas in human language. It was written by human men. These men were inspired of the Holy Spirit. Because of the imperfections of human understanding of language, or the perversity of the human mind, ingenious in evading truth, many read and understand the Bible to please themselves. It is not that the difficulty is in the Bible. Opposing politicians argue points of law in the statute book, and take opposite views in their application and in these laws.

The Scriptures were given to men, not in a continuous chain of unbroken utterances, but piece by piece through successive generations, as God in His providence saw a fitting opportunity to impress man at sundry times and divers places. Men wrote as they were moved upon by the Holy Ghost. There is "first the bud, then the blossom, and next the fruit," "first the blade, then the ear, after that the full corn in the ear." This is exactly what the Bible utterances are to us.

There is not always perfect order or apparent unity in the Scriptures. The miracles of Christ are not given in exact order, but are given just as the circumstances occurred, which called for this divine revealing of the power of Christ. The truths of the Bible are as pearls hidden. They must be searched, dug out by painstaking effort. Those who take only a surface view of the Scriptures will, with their superficial knowledge, which they think is very deep, talk of the contradictions of the Bible, and question the authority of the Scriptures. But those whose hearts are in harmony with truth and duty will search the Scriptures with a heart prepared to receive divine impressions. The illuminated soul sees a spiritual unity, one grand golden thread running through the whole, but it requires patience, thought, and prayer to trace out the precious golden thread. Sharp contentions over the Bible have led to investigation and revealed the precious jewels of truth. Many tears have been shed, many prayers offered, that the Lord would open the understanding to His Word.

The Bible is not given to us in grand superhuman language. Jesus, in order to reach man where he is, took humanity. The Bible must be given in the language of men. Everything that is human is imperfect. Different meanings are expressed by the same word; there is not one word for each distinct idea. The Bible was given for practical purposes.

The stamps of minds are different. All do not understand expressions and statements alike. Some understand the statements of the Scriptures to suit their own particular minds and cases. Prepossessions, prejudices, and passions have a strong influence to darken the understanding and confuse the mind even in reading the words of Holy Writ.

The disciples traveling to Emmaus needed to be disentangled in their interpretation of the Scriptures. Jesus walked with them disguised, and as a man, He talked with them. Beginning at Moses and the prophets He taught them in all things concerning Himself, that His life, His mission, His sufferings, His death were just as the Word of God had foretold. He opened their understanding that they might understand the Scriptures. How quickly He straightened out the tangled ends and showed the unity and divine verity of the Scriptures. How much men in these times need their understanding opened.

The Bible is written by inspired men, but it is not God's mode of thought and expression. It is that of humanity. God, as a writer, is not represented. Men will often say such an expression is not like God. But God has not put Himself in words, in logic, in rhetoric, on trial in the Bible. The writers of the Bible were God's penmen, not His pen. Look at the different writers.

It is not the words of the Bible that are inspired, but the men that were inspired. Inspiration acts not on the man's words or his expressions but on the man himself, who, under the influence of the Holy Ghost, is imbued with thoughts. But the words receive the impress of the individual mind. The divine mind is diffused. The divine mind and will is combined with the human mind and will; **thus the utterances of the man are the word of God.** (Ellen G. White manuscript 24, 1886; White, *Selected Messages*, Vol. 1, p. 19–21; emphasis added)

CHAPTER 1

The Conspiracy

"For we are not as many, which corrupt the word of God: but as of sincerity, but as of God, in the sight of God speak we in Christ" (2 Cor. 2:17, KJV).

Most Christians believe in the providential preservation of the Bible. There are scriptures such as Psalm 12:6–7, 119:89, 111, 152, Ecclesiastes 3:14, Matthew 24:35, and 1 Peter 1:23–25 from the Authorized Version that let us know God has preserved His Word down through the ages to our present time. Providential preservation is as essential in preserving the pure words of God as divine inspiration was for giving them in the first place.

However, from scriptures like Revelation 22:18–19, 2 Corinthians 2:17 and 4:2 it is understood that providential preservation does not mean that attempts would not be made to alter the Word of God. It more communicates that those attempts would not be successful. Just as God raised up reformers to bring His church through the Dark Ages, He has raised up watchmen in our day to alert the church to Satan's attacks on the Holy Word.

Because God knew that evil angels would conspire with wicked men to corrupt His word He included fearful warnings like this one taken from the book of Revelation:

> For I testify unto every man that heareth the words of the prophecy of this book, If any man shall add unto these things, God shall add unto him the plagues that are written in this book: And if any man shall take away from the words of the book of this prophecy, God shall take away his part out of the book of life, and out of the holy city, and from the things which are written in this book. (Rev. 22:18–19, KJV)

Ellen White, speaking of the warning in Revelation 22:18 and 19, said:

> Such are the warnings which God has given to guard men against changing in any manner that which He has revealed or commanded. These solemn denunciations apply to all who by their influence lead men to regard lightly the law of God. They should cause those to fear and tremble who flippantly declare it a matter of little consequence whether we obey God's law or not. All who exalt their own opinions above divine revelation, all who would change the plain meaning of Scripture to suit their own convenience, or for the sake of conforming to the world, are taking upon themselves a fearful responsibility. The written word, the law of God, will measure the character of every man and condemn all whom this unerring test shall declare wanting. (White, *The Great Controversy*, p. 268)

Satan hates the word of God and has made war upon it since the beginning of his rebellion in heaven.

According to Revelation 19:13, John 1:1, and 1 John 5:7, Jesus Christ is the incarnate Word of God. He is the Living Word. Satan made war upon the Living Word in heaven: Revelation 12:7 and Isaiah 14:12–14. He made war upon the Living Word on earth: Revelation 12:3–4, Matthew 4:1–10, Matthew 16:21–23, and *Desire of Ages*, p. 686.5. Satan has attacked the written word of God overtly as well as covertly throughout history: Jeremiah 36, Deuteronomy 12:8, Judges 17:6, 21:25, 2 Kings 22:8, and 2 Chronicles 34:14. He has also attacked the spoken word as well as those who spoke the word: Genesis 3:1, 1 Kings 22:13–28, Jeremiah 38:1–6, and Hebrews 11:37. Satan began waging his war upon the Word of God through deception: Revelation 12:9. As the war upon the Word of God began, so it will continue to the close of time—deception will be the principal weapon employed by the arch deceiver.

One of Satan's principle deceptions has been to lead people to believe that something decidedly different could be the same. There is an overabundance of modern Bible versions in the marketplace today that change keywords in the Bible, thereby changing also the original meaning as well as some doctrinal text of the Protestant Bible. The average person calling himself a Christian today does not read the Bible but depends on "ecclesiastical men" to decide for them what to believe. The fact that modern Bible versions differ remarkably from the Authorized Version goes, for the most part, unnoticed. The September 2012 edition of *Christianity Today*, in the section entitled "Gleanings," reports that more than eighty percent (80%) of Protestants do not read their Bibles regularly.

Before continuing it is important to note the differences between a Bible version, a translation of a version, and a Bible paraphrase. A Bible version is a Bible translated directly from the language it was originally written in into another language. A translation of a Bible version into another language is simply called a translation. A paraphrased Bible restates text or passages in another form or other words, often to clarify meaning. Paraphrases are purely the understanding or opinions of its author(s).

The Authorized King James Version compilers translated from the Majority Text and the Textus Receptus stream. The Textus Receptus is based on the vast majority (90%) of the 5000+ Greek manuscripts and codices in existence. Virtually all of the other English Bible translations spring from the minority manuscripts or codices initially translated by Fenton John Anthony Hort and Brooke Foss Westcott and later updated by Eberhard Nestle and Kurt Aland.

Nearly all modern English Bible versions rely primarily on the Greek text initially translated by Westcott and Hort, later legitimized by Nestle/Aland. The minority manuscripts were inferior to the Textus Receptus, and at least one of its principle codices is suspected by many scholars to be a forgery. Westcott and Hort, the principle and most notable of the 1881 Bible revision committee of the Revised Version, used what has come to be known as the Critical Text. Though the Critical Text translations are based on inferior codices, for reasons that defy logic, modern-day biblical scholars consider them to be more reliable than the Textus Receptus. A procedure that has come to be known as Dynamic Equivalence was used to translate the corrupted codices and was later used in the creation of the Nestle/Aland Greek text. The principle two codices used were the Vaticanus B and the Codex Sinaiticus (Aleph).

Dynamic Equivalence, also known as Functional Equivalence, is nothing more than a fancy name for paraphrase. It attempts to convey the thought expressed in a text as opposed to what the text says. Eugene A. Nida (1914–2011), author of *Toward A Science of Translating With Special Reference To Principles And Procedures Involved In Bible Translating*, became the chief advocate and user of Dynamic Equivalency. Nida believed the Scriptures themselves were not inspired, that God did not inspire words but concepts. This belief is also known as "concept inspiration." Nida promoted the idea that those who believed in the translation of words were guilty of "worshiping words more than worshiping God." Incidentally, he was also an adjunct professor at the Pontifical Gregorian University in Rome, Italy.

It's interesting that many Protestants have come to believe something very similar—God inspires concepts, not words, and those words are subject to change at the whims of supposedly more sophisticated men. It is this fallacy, that God inspired mere concepts rather than words or men, that has opened the floodgates for the modern Bible version entrance into the churches.

Dynamic Equivalence is, in fact, the interpretations of men. It can be essentially said of all modern Bible versions, because almost all of them are the product of the Nestle/Aland Greek translations, are the product of man's devising and not God's. The King James Bible translators used the Formal Equivalence method for translating the King James Bible. Formal Equivalence attempts to render the text word-for-word, even at the expense of the natural expression of the English language. This process allows the Holy Spirit to be the interpreter as opposed to men.

"The movement for a revision of the Authorized Version of the Holy Scriptures commenced on May 6, 1870, in the Convocation of Canterbury. An influential committee was at once formed, consisting mainly of distinguished scholars and divines within the pale of the Established Church, but with power to consult or add to their number eminent Biblical scholars of all denominations" (D.B. Loughran, *Bible Versions – Which is the Real Word of God?* http://1ref.us/nk, accessed June 26, 2018). The Seventh-day Adventist Church was in its infancy in America at that time and would not have been included on that committee had it been a well-known denomination. Seventh-day Adventist Bible scholars have never served on any subsequent Bible revision committee since men decided the Word of God needed revision.

B.F. Westcott and F.J.A. Hort were believers in evolution, ghosts, and Roman Catholic theology and philosophy. They were members of secret societies and were also spiritualists. At best Westcott and Hort were Roman Catholic sympathizers, at worst Jesuits, posing as Protestants to gain acceptance for their Bible revisions by the Protestant world. They appear to have had quite a bit of success with their conspiracy to unsettle confidence in the King James Authorized Bible as these spurious modern Bibles permeate most of the Protestant churches today.

"Dr. Henry M Morris, a founding father of the Institute for Creation Research, USA, made these telling comments concerning modern translators" (D.B. Loughran, *Bible Versions—Which is the Real Word of God?*, p. 36):

> As far as the Hebrew text developed by Rudolph Kittel is concerned, it is worth noting that Kittel was a German rationalist higher critic, rejecting Biblical inerrancy and firmly devoted to evolutionism. The men most responsible for alterations in the New Testament text were B.F. Westcott and F.J.A. Hort, whose Greek New Testament was largely updated by Eberhard Nestle and Kurt Aland. All these men were evolutionists. Furthermore, Westcott and Hort denied Biblical inerrancy and promoted spiritism and racism. Nestle and Aland, like Kittel, were German theological skeptics.
>
> Westcott and Hort were also the most influential members of the English revision committee, which produced the English Revised Version of the Bible. The corresponding American revision committee, which developed the American Standard Version of 1901, was headed by another liberal evolutionist, Philip Schaff. Most new versions since that time have adopted the same presuppositions as those of the 19th century revisers ...
>
> So one of the serious problems with most modern English translations is that they rely heavily on Hebrew and Greek manuscripts of the Bible developed by liberals, rationalists, and evolutionists ... Is this how God would preserve His word? Would he not more likely have used devout scholars who believed in the absolute inerrancy and authority of the Bible? ...

The following quotes are a small sampling from *Life and Letters of Brooke Foss Westcott*, sometime Bishop of Durham, and *Life and Letters of Fenton John Anthony Hort*. Written by Arthur Westcott and Fenton John Anthony Hort respectively, these volumes containing their writings about themselves should be conclusive evidence of their infidelity in creating a trustworthy revision of the King James Bible, regardless of their sincerity in translating or their possible repentance afterwards.

Brooke Foss Westcott

Writing from France to his fiancée in 1847:

> After leaving the monastery we shaped our course to a little oratory which we discovered on the summit of a neighbouring hill, and by a little scrambling we reached it. Fortunately we found the door open. It is very small, with one kneeling-place; and behind a screen was a "Pieta" the size of life (i.e. a Virgin and dead Christ). The sculpture was painted, and such a group in such a place and at such a time was deeply impressive. I could not help thinking on the fallen grandeur of the Romish Church, on her zeal even in error, on her earnestness and self-devotion, which we might, with nobler views and a purer end, strive to imitate. **Had I been alone I could have knelt there for hours**. (p. 81)

To the Archbishop of Canterbury, March 4, 1890:

> No one now, I suppose holds that the first three chapters of Genesis, for example, gives a literal history—I could never understand how any one reading them with open eyes could think they did—yet they disclose to us a Gospel. So it is probably elsewhere. (Vol. II, p. 69; http://1ref.us/nu, accessed June 26, 2018; page 89 in the pdf)

Writing to Hort September 29th:

> As to our proposed recension of the New Testament text, our object would be, I suppose, to prepare a text for common and general use ... **with such an end in view, would it not be best to introduce only certain emendations into the received text, and to note in the margin such as seem likely or noticeable**—after Griesbach's manner? ... I feel most keenly the disgrace of circulating what I feel to be falsified copies of the Holy Scripture [a reference to the KJV], and am most anxious to provide something to replace them. **This cannot be any text resting solely on our own judgment, even if we were not too inexperienced to make one; but it must be supported by a clear and obvious preponderance of evidence.** The margin will give ample scope for our own ingenuity or principles ... my wish would be to leave the popular received text except where it is clearly wrong. (Westcott, *Life and Letters of Brooke Foss Westcott*, Vol. I., p. 228–229)

In his book *An Understandable History Of The Bible*, Samuel C. Gipp has this to say about Westcott (Loughran, *Bible Versions—Which is the Real Word of God?*, p. 34):

> We have in Brooke Foss Westcott a man who believed in communal living; a man who believed that the second coming of Christ was spiritual, heaven was a state of the mind, prayers for the dead were permissible in private devotions, and that Christ came to bring peace through international disarmament. He believed in purgatory and admiration for Mary, and he thought the Bible was like any other book.
>
> This is the man who walked into the Revision Committee and sat in judgment of our Bible. He thought he saw room for

improvement in the Authorized Version and offered a pro-Roman Greek text with which to correct it.

The ironic thing is that Bible-believing Christians, educators and preachers, who would never agree with his theology, have for years exalted his opinion of the Greek as nearly infallible. These facts alone should be reason enough to condemn Westcott and Hort, their Greek Text and the MSS which they used to arrive at such a text. But let us look at their actions concerning the molesting of the pure words of the King James Bible, in favour of Rome. Saddest of all, we have in Brooke Foss Westcott a man who neither believed in salvation by grace nor ever experienced it. There is no record in his 'Life and Letters' that he ever accepted Christ as his personal Saviour. (Gipp, *An Understandable History of The Bible*)

Fenton John Anthony Hort

Writing to Westcott, March 10, 1860:

Have you read Darwin? How I should like a talk with you about it! In spite of difficulties, I am inclined to think it unanswerable. In any case, it is a treat to read such a book. (Vol. I, p. 414)

Writing to Westcott August 14, 1860:

"It is of course true that we can only know God through human forms, but then I think the whole Bible echoes the language of Genesis 1:27 and so assures us that human forms are divine forms." (Vol. I, p. 445)

Writing to Westcott October 15, 1860:

> "I entirely agree—correcting one word—with what you there say on the Atonement, having for many years believed that 'the absolute union of the Christian (or rather, of man) with Christ Himself' is the spiritual truth of which the popular doctrine of substitution is an immoral and material counterfeit ... Certainly nothing can be more unscriptural than the modern limiting of Christ's bearing our sins and sufferings to His death; but indeed that is only one aspect of an almost universal heresy." (Vol. I, p. 430)

Writing to Mr. H. Brinton, January, 1886, Referring to Article IX of the 39 Articles of the Anglican Church:

> The authors of the Article doubtless assumed the strictly historical character of the account of the Fall in Genesis. This assumption is now, in my belief, no longer reasonable. But the early chapters of Genesis remain a divinely appointed parable or apologue setting forth important practical truths on subjects which, as matter of history, lie outside our present ken. (Vol. II, p. 329)
>
> Westcott, Gorham, C. B. Scott, Bensons, Bradshaw, Laud, etc. and I have started a society for the investigation of ghosts and all supernatural appearances and effects, being disposed to believe that such things really exist. (Vol. I, p. 211)
>
> This may sound cowardice—I have a craving that our text should be cast upon the world before we deal with matters likely to brand us with suspicion. I mean a text issued by men who are already know for what will undoubtedly be treated as dangerous heresy will have great difficulty in finding its way to regions which it might otherwise hope to reach and whence

it would not be easily banished by subsequent alarms. (Vol I, p. 445)

> No rational being doubts the need of a revised Bible; and the popular practical objections are worthless. Yet I have an increasing feeling in favor of delay. Of course, no revision can be final, and it would be absurd to wait for perfection. But the criticism of both Testaments in text and interpretation alike, appears to me to be just now in that chaotic state (in Germany hardly if at all less than in England), that the results of immediate revision would be peculiarly unsatisfactory. ... 1 John 5:7 might be got rid of in a month; and if that were done, I should prefer to wait a few years. (Vol. II, p. 128)

July 7, 1870:

> It is quite impossible to judge the value of what appear to be trifling alterations merely by reading them one after another. Taken together, they have often important bearings which few would think of a first. There is but one safe rule, to be as scrupulously exact as possible, remembering, of course, that there is a truth of tone as well as of grammar and dictionary. The difference between a picture say of Raffaelle and a feeble copy of it is made up of a number of trivial differences. (Hort, *Life and Letters of Fenton John Anthony Hort*, Vol. II, p. 138)

The letters written by Westcott and Hort should be enough to convince astute readers that they could not have been Protestant Christians in the truest sense of the word. They hated the Protestant Bible and set about trying to unsettle faith in it.

CHAPTER 2

Spurious Bible Versions

"If the foundations be destroyed, what can the righteous do?" (Ps. 11:3, KJV).

"Most wondrous book! bright candle of the Lord! Star of eternity! The only light by which the bark of man can navigate the sea of life, and gain the coast of bliss securely."

Why should not this book—this precious treasure—be exalted and esteemed as a valued friend? This is our chart across the stormy sea of life. It is our guide-book, showing us the way to the eternal mansions, and the character we must have to inhabit them. There is no book the perusal of which will so elevate and strengthen the mind as the study of the Bible. Here the intellect will find themes of the most elevated character to call out its powers. There is nothing that will so endow with vigor all our faculties as bringing them in contact with the stupendous truths of revelation. The effort to grasp and measure these great thoughts expands the mind. We may dig down deep into the mine of truth, and gather precious treasures with which to enrich the soul. Here we may learn the true way to live, the safe way to die.

A familiar acquaintance with the Scriptures sharpens the discerning powers, and fortifies the soul against the attacks of Satan. The Bible is the sword of the Spirit, which will never fail to vanquish the adversary. It is the only true guide in all matters of faith and practice. The reason why Satan has so great control over the minds and hearts of men is that they have not made the Word of God the man of their counsel, and all their ways have not been tried by the true test. The Bible will show us what course we must pursue to become heirs of glory.

As the heart is opened to the entrance of the Word, light from the throne of God will shine into the soul. That Word, cherished in the heart, will yield to the student a treasure of knowledge that is priceless. Its ennobling principles will stamp the character with honesty and truthfulness, temperance and integrity. (White, *Our High Calling*, p. 31)

> *There is nothing that will so endow with vigor all our faculties as bringing them in contact with the stupendous truths of revelation.*

The Lord God in His infinite wisdom and mercy has seen fit to give to us the Scriptures in a language we can read and understand. For those of us who are English speakers, it is this author's firm belief that that Bible is the Authorized King James Version.

Many people believe that a selection of the Bible they use or the Bible that others use is purely a matter of personal preference. However, let us evaluate that line of thinking for a moment: What if one chose the

Queen James Bible, the Bible that supports the homosexual movement's agenda; or the Kanye West Bible, or even the Action Bible, a Bible in comic book form. The question must be answered, are these legitimate Bibles or clever counterfeits?

The anonymous creators of the *Queen James Bible* made the following assertions:

> Homosexuality was first mentioned in the Bible in 1946 in the Revised Standard Version. There is no mention of or reference to homosexuality in any Bible prior to this—only interpretations have been made. Anti-LGBT Bible interpretations commonly cite only eight verses in the Bible that they interpret to mean homosexuality is a sin; Eight verses in a book of thousands!
>
> The Queen James Bible seeks to resolve interpretive ambiguity in the Bible as it pertains to homosexuality: We edited those eight verses in a way that makes homophobic interpretations impossible. (http://1ref.us/nl, accessed June 26, 2018)

Here are two examples of the changes made to suit their agenda:

Leviticus 18:22, Queen James Version:
"Thou shalt not lie with mankind as with womankind **in the temple of Molech**; it is an abomination" (QJV, p. 75, http://1ref.us/nl, accessed June 26, 2018).

Leviticus 20:13, QJV:
"If a man also lie with mankind **in the temple of Molech**, as he lieth with a woman, both of them have committed an abomination: they shall surely be put to death" (QJV, p. 76, http://1ref.us/nl, accessed June 26, 2018).

For those of us who believe that the Bible is the inspired Word of God, this is a blasphemous self-serving attempt at reducing God's Word to the suppositions of men. The irony here is that many in their attempts to discredit the authenticity of the King James Bible claim that King James I was a homosexual. Although that is debatable, it is ironic that those who hoped that by vilifying his name the Bible that bore it would be tarnished. It is amazing that those who believe the Bible is not the inspired Word of God, but merely contrived by men would believe that a gay man would authorize a Bible that condemns that very practice.

Here are those same two Scriptures from above as they appear in the King James Bible:

Leviticus 18:22, KJV:
"Thou shalt not lie with mankind, as with womankind: it is abomination."

Leviticus 20:13, KJV:
"If a man also lie with mankind, as he lieth with a woman, both of them have committed an abomination: they shall surely be put to death; their blood shall be upon them."

Notice how the words "in the temple of Molech" were added to give the impression that a homosexual act is only sinful if practiced in a pagan temple or in a pagan worship ceremony. It is not the intent or scope of this book to delve into the Greek or Hebrew to determine or second guess the choice of words the King James translators used. However, it should be noted that the Majority Manuscripts do not contain the words "temple of Molech."

Some may be thinking at this point, "What's the big deal?" So what if the writers of the Kanye West Bible, the comic book Bible, and even the Queen James Bible produced a Bible that promotes their agenda. After all, every Christian knows that and will avoid any such Bible. Would they? Most Christians believe or believed at one time that the New World Translation, the Jehovah's Witness Bible is a corrupted translation created to promote a belief system that denies the deity of Jesus Christ. The fact that the New International Version and the New King James Version being the most purchased Bibles in the world after the King James Authorized Bible prove that most Christians do not know what they claim to believe.

The NIV, for example, has all the changes of the New World Translation and then some. The NKJV also supports many of the textual changes in both the NIV and the NWT, and most Christians are not any the wiser.

The NIV did the same thing with 1 Kings 14:24, 1 Kings 5:12, 1 Kings 22:46; Deut. 23:17; and 2 Kings 23:7 as the Queen James Bible did with the verses in Leviticus. The text is worded to give the impression that the practice of homosexuality is only sinful when associated with paganism.

1 Kings 14:24, NIV:

"There were even male **shrine prostitutes** in the land; the people engaged in all the detestable practices of the nations the LORD had driven out before the Israelites."

1 Kings 14:24, KJV:

"And there were also **sodomites** in the land: and they did according to all the abominations of the nations which the LORD cast out before the children of Israel."

Though the NIV and other modern translations using the critical Greek text may use accurate synonyms and/or alternative wording, the English understanding of the verse is altered, and even doctrine is changed, as a result. For instance, sodomites/sodomite do not appear in the NIV. Those words make it abundantly clear that the practice of homosexuality in any form or location is an abomination in the sight of God. It is obvious, from texts like these, that God finds some sins more abhorrent than others. He loves all sinners enough to warn them away from any practice that will bar them from the courts of heaven. While it is true that some are calling themselves Christians have placed obstacles in the paths of those practicing sexual sins by misrepresenting God, it is equally true that God has placed in His word the provisions for salvation. We are to follow Christ and not a man; we are to look to His word for instruction. That is why it is imperative to have the right Bible.

CHAPTER 3

Unmasking the NKJV and the NASB

"Cease, my son, to hear the instruction that causeth to err from the words of knowledge" (Prov. 19:27, KJV).

The NASB Scandal

Some biblical scholars insist that the New American Standard Bible (NASB) is the best Bible translation in existence. That sentiment is even echoed in nearly all Christian institutions of higher learning and churches alike. It has been said that the NASB:

> Is a literal translation, attempting to take each word or phrase and give it the most literal word for word counterpart available. It does not take the modern politically correct route of making all references to God, men, and women "gender-inclusive" (as the NRSV is known for). Compared to the other more popular translations, the NIV and the NRSV, the NASB time and

time again offers the better translation. (*A Case for the NASB*, http://1ref.us/no, accessed June 26, 2018)

Similar statements are also made in favor of the New King James Version. But is this true? These are the usual selling points for modern Bible versions. Many Christians repeat these slogans as if they had done actual research on Bible versions. The sad reality is most Christians are oblivious to the fact that there is a Bible controversy at all.

> "Frank Logsdon (1907–1987) was a major contributor in the development of the New American Standard Bible (NASB). He was friend with F. Dewey Lockman (1942–1974, President & Founder of the Lockman Foundation), and was involved in a feasibility study involving purchasing the copyright of the American Standard Version (ASV) with Lockman that led to the eventual production of the NASB. He interviewed some of the translators and even wrote the preface to the translation. He eventually became aware that there was something wrong with the NASB and rejected it. He later became a promoter of the KJV. Logsdon made this statement concerning the NASB:
>
> I must under God denounce every attachment to the New American Standard Version. I'm afraid I'm in trouble with the Lord … We laid the groundwork; I wrote the format; I helped interview some of the translators; I sat with the translator; I wrote the preface. When you see the preface to the New American Standard, those are my words … it's wrong, it's terribly wrong; it's frightfully wrong … I'm in trouble; … I can no longer ignore these criticisms I am hearing and I can't refute them. The deletions are absolutely frightening … there are so many. The finest leaders that we have today haven't gone into it just as I hadn't gone into it … that's how easily one can be deceived … Are we so naive that we do not suspect Satanic deception in

all of this?" (*Defend and Proclaim the Faith*, http://1ref.us/nm, accessed June 26, 2018)

No doubt when you, the reader, look to verify the validity of the above quote you will encounter information designed to discredit Frank Logsdon typical of most smear campaigns.

The NKJV Debacle

Among Satan's greatest counterfeits is the New King James Version. Christians that would never touch a New International Version, Revised Standard, the Message Bible, or any of the other versions, are being "seduced" by the subtle NKJV. The title alone is extremely deceptive causing the unsuspecting believer to buy what is essentially a counterfeit of the Authorized Version, the Word of God.

In his book *Final Authority*, author William P. Grady says this concerning the NKJV:

> From 1611 to 1881, God's foot soldiers wielded KJV swords while defending spiritual barley fields against Jesuits armed with Douay-Rheims Versions. Their grip grew tighter from 1881–1974 as one Alexandrian impostor after another was driven from the field. Suddenly, a profit-oriented corporation (the same crown who manufactured the enemies swords) would prevail upon the church to believe that the Holy Spirit had abruptly ordered a weapon change - in the very **heat of the battle**! Their corrupt rendering of Romans 1:25 says it best. Instead of KJV's '**changed**' we read, '**exchanged** the truth of God for a lie.' A true believer will never exchange his KJV for a NKJV. The reason for this resistance is the same today as it was in Bible days. With his very life at stake, the grip of the ancient warrior was so intense that warm water was often needed

at battle's end to literally pry the weapon from his cramped hands. A person with an ounce of spiritual discernment can see that He who **'is not the author of confusion'** would never pick such timing to introduce yet another English revision! The outstanding distinction of a spiritual warrior will always be that, **his hand clave unto the sword** ...

The truth of the matter is that the New King James Version represents Satan's ultimate deception to oppose God's remnant in the closing days of the New Testament age. Having enlisted the lukewarm materialist with his **NIV**, the devil sets a trap for the diligent soul winner with the **NKJV**. Although his worldly counterparts embraced the **oldest is best** theory of manuscript evidences, the true Bible believer refused to abandon the **Majority Text**, retaining the Divine commendation of, **'thou has kept my word.'** Thus we find Satan attempting to wean him away from his Authorised Version with the deceitful half-step of a generic look-alike, **TRANSLATED FROM THE TRUSTWORTHY TEXTUS RECEPTUS!** ...

Conservative estimates of the total translation changes in the **NKJV** are generally put at over **100,000**! This is an average of 82 changes for each of the 1219 pages in the **NKJV** ... Along this line of abuse, the most shocking revelation about the 'New' King James Version is that it is literally laced with **'old'** readings from the **Revised Standard** and **New American Standard Versions**. This revival of Alexandrian readings is one of the best-kept secrets of the decade. Whenever there is a marked departure from the text of the **KJV**, the alternative reading is frequently taken from either the **RSV**, **NASV**, or oftentimes, both. For instance, in the first chapter of John's Gospel, there are 51 verses. Of this total, 45 (or 88%) have been altered by the **NKJV**. Among this number, 34 (75%) exhibit a distinct **RSV** or **NASV** reading while 6 show a partial reading. Only

5 (15%) appear unique to the **NKJV**. (Loughran, David B., *Bible Versions, Which is the Real Word of God*, p. 55)

Although the New King James does bear a "likeness" to the King James Bible, as does the NASB, if you keep reading you'll soon see diabolical changes that alter doctrine. Many scholars argue that doctrine in modern Bible versions remain unchanged as a result of changing the language construction. However, we are about to discover that is just not true:

> The Preface to the NKJV reads, "A special feature of the New King James Version is its conformity to the thought flow of the 1611 Bible ... the new edition, while much clearer are so close to the traditional ..." As we delve into the reasons why this statement is blatantly false, to anyone who would take the time to compare, let us first consider the NKJV claims to make the "old" KJV "much clearer" by "updating obsolete words" (New King James Version, 1982e., p. 1235).
>
> The Preface to the NKJV states, "...thee, thou, and ye are replaced by the simple you ... These pronouns are no longer part of our language." But "thee, thou and ye" were "no longer part of the language" during 1611 either (just read the intro to the 1611 King James, there are no "thee," "thou" and "ye"). In fact, Webster's Third New International Dictionary, says of ye: "used from the earliest of times to the late 13th century ..." (p. 2648). And yet the 1611 King James was published 400 years later in the 17th century! So why are they there?
>
> The Greek and Hebrew languages contain a different word for the second person singular and the second person plural pronouns. Today we use the one-word "you" for both the singular and plural. But because the translators of the 1611 King James Bible desired an accurate, word-for-word translation of the Hebrew and Greek text, they could NOT use the one-word

"you" throughout! If it begins with "t" (thou, thy, thine), it's SINGULAR, but if it begins with "y" (ye), it's PLURAL. Ads for the NKJV call it "the Accurate One," and yet the 1611 King James, by using "thee," "thou," and "ye," is far more accurate!

By the way, if the "thee's" and "thou's" are "… no longer part of our language," why aren't the NKJV translators rushing to make our hymnbooks "much clearer"? "How Great Thou Art" to "How Great You Are," or "Come Thou Fount" to "Come You Fount." Doesn't sound right, does it? Isn't it amazing that they wouldn't dare "correct" our hymns—and yet, without the slightest hesitation—they'll "correct" the word of God! (Unknown Author)

A careful reading of the KJV would reveal that the translators used the word "you" exclusively in the plural sense as not to confuse the plural with the singular as the modern versions do. In the following example, the King James translators employed the archaic words thee, thy, and thou to convey the original Greek thought in Luke 22:31 and 32, that Jesus was speaking to Peter about Satan's desire to destroy all of the disciples (you, Greek word "humas"). You, ye, your, and yours were used exclusively in their plural form by the King James translators. Then He informs Peter (thee, Greek word "sou") to strengthen his (thy, genitive case of the Greek word "sou") brethren when he is converted. The New King James Version leads one to believe that Jesus is only speaking of Satan's desire to destroy Peter by using the plural (you) to mean singular Peter. As stated above, the KJV translators use the word "you" exclusively in the plural sense.

Luke 22:31–32, KJV:
"And the Lord said, Simon, Simon, behold, Satan hath desired to have **you** (all of the disciples), that he may sift **you** (all of the disciples) as wheat: But I have prayed for **thee (Peter)**, that **thy (Peter)** faith fail not: and when **thou (Peter)** art converted, strengthen **thy (Peter)** brethren."

Luke 22:31–32, NKJV:

"And the Lord said, 'Simon, Simon! Indeed, Satan has asked for **you**, that he may sift **you** as wheat. But I have prayed for **you**, that **your** faith should not fail; and when **you** have returned to Me, strengthen **your** brethren.'"

Our Protestant understanding of John 3:7 referring to the new birth experience comes from the King James Bible. In that verse Jesus, addressing Nicodemus with the pronoun "thee," tells him that "ye" must be born again. If the word "you" is used here, as it is in modern versions, it appears that only Nicodemus is required to be born again. The doctrine of the new birth experience held by most Protestants is made nonexistent.

Another example of how the modern Bible versions distort what the Holy Spirit desires to communicate can also be found in Joshua 1:1–9 of the New King James Version. Notice how one cannot distinguish when God is speaking about Joshua or when He was speaking about the children of Israel. Because the NKJV translators replaced the singular thee and thou, when God was speaking of Joshua to the plural 'you,' it becomes confusing to the reader who is being referred to in this chapter—Joshua or Israel. And we know that God is not the author of confusion.

Joshua 1:1–9, KJV:

> Now after the death of Moses the servant of the LORD it came to pass, that the LORD spake unto Joshua the son of Nun, Moses' minister, saying, Moses my servant is dead; now therefore arise, go over this Jordan, **thou**, and all this people, unto the land which I do give to them, even to the children of Israel. Every place that the sole of **your** foot shall tread upon, that have I given unto **you**, as I said unto Moses. From the wilderness and this Lebanon even unto the great river, the river Euphrates, all the land of the Hittites, and unto the great sea toward the going down of the sun, shall be **your** coast. There shall not any man be able to stand before **thee** all the days of thy life: as I was with Moses, so I will be with **thee**: I will not

fail **thee**, nor forsake **thee**. Be strong and of a good courage: for unto this people shalt **thou** divide for an inheritance the land, which I sware unto their fathers to give them. Only be **thou** strong and very courageous, that **thou** mayest observe to do according to all the law, which Moses my servant commanded **thee**: turn not from it to the right hand or to the left, that **thou** mayest prosper whithersoever **thou** goest. This book of the law shall not depart out of thy mouth; but **thou** shalt meditate therein day and night, that **thou** mayest observe to do according to all that is written therein: for then **thou** shalt make **thy** way prosperous, and then **thou** shalt have good success. Have not I commanded **thee**? Be strong and of a good courage; be not afraid, neither be **thou** dismayed: for the LORD **thy** God is with **thee** whithersoever **thou** goest.

Joshua 1:1–9, NKJV:

After the death of Moses the servant of the LORD, it came to pass that the LORD spoke to Joshua the son of Nun, Moses' assistant, saying: "Moses My servant is dead. Now therefore, arise, go over this Jordan, **you** and all this people, to the land which I am giving to them—the children of Israel. Every place that the sole of **your** foot will tread upon I have given **you**, as I said to Moses. From the wilderness and this Lebanon as far as the great river, the River Euphrates, all the land of the Hittites, and to the Great Sea toward the going down of the sun, shall be **your** territory. No man shall be able to stand before **you** all the days of **your** life; as I was with Moses, so I will be with **you**. I will not leave **you** nor forsake **you**. Be strong and of good courage, for to this people **you** shall divide as an inheritance the land which I swore to their fathers to give them. Only be strong and very courageous, that **you** may observe to do according to all the law which Moses My servant commanded **you**; do not turn from it to the right hand or to the left, that **you** may prosper wherever **you** go. This Book of the Law shall not depart from your mouth, but **you** shall meditate in it day and night, that **you** may observe to do according to all that is written in it. For then **you** will make your way prosperous, and then **you** will have good success. Have I not commanded **you**? Be strong and of good courage; do not be afraid, nor be dismayed, for the LORD your God is with **you** wherever you go."

CHAPTER 4

Precept Upon Precept Line Upon Line

"Study to shew thyself approved unto God, a workman that needeth not to be ashamed, rightly dividing the word of truth" (2 Tim. 2:15, KJV).

The Bible truly is its own expositor. There are even texts, Isaiah 28:7–13 that supply us with the method for rightly dividing the word of truth. Of course, the modern versions destroy this method by replacing crucial keywords, which we will see in a moment. But first let us look at how The Spirit of Prophecy, in *Testimonies to Ministers and Gospel Workers* unfold truths found in the King James Version of these texts:

> Those who are in responsible positions are not to become converted to the self-indulgent, extravagant principles of the world, for they cannot afford it; and if they could, Christlike principles would not allow it. Manifold teaching needs to be given. "Whom shall He teach knowledge? and whom shall He make to understand doctrine? them that are weaned from

the milk, and drawn from the breasts. For precept must be upon precept, precept upon precept; line upon line, line upon line; here a little, and there a little." Thus the word of the Lord is patiently to be brought before the children and kept before them, by parents who believe the word of God. "For with stammering lips and another tongue will He speak to this people. To whom He said, This is the rest wherewith ye may cause the weary to rest; and this is the refreshing: yet they would not hear. But the word of the Lord was unto them precept upon precept, precept upon precept; line upon line, line upon line; here a little, and there a little; that they might go, and fall backward, and be broken, and snared, and taken." Why?—because they did not heed the word of the Lord that came unto them.

This means those who have not received instruction, but have cherished their own wisdom, and have chosen to work themselves according to their own ideas. The Lord gives these the test, that they shall either take their position to follow His counsel, or refuse and do according to their own ideas, and then the Lord will leave them to the sure result. In all our ways, in all our service to God, He speaks to us, "Give Me thine heart." It is the submissive, teachable spirit that God wants. That which gives to prayer its excellence is the fact that it is breathed from a loving, obedient heart.

It is the submissive, teachable spirit that God wants.

God requires certain things of His people; if they say, I will not give up my heart to do this thing, the Lord lets them go on in their supposed wise judgment without heavenly wisdom, until this scripture [Isaiah 28:13 "But the word of the LORD was unto them precept upon precept, precept upon precept; line upon line, line upon line; here a little, and there a little; that they might go, and fall backward, and be broken, and snared, and taken.] is fulfilled. You are not to say, I will follow the Lord's guidance up to a certain point that is in harmony with my judgment, and then hold fast to your own ideas, refusing to be molded after the Lord's similitude. Let the question be asked, Is this the will of the Lord? not, Is this the opinion or judgment of—? (White, *Testimonies to Ministers and Gospel Workers*, p. 418–419)

The Spirit of Prophecy not only unfolds the proper teaching/study methods of Isaiah 28:7–13 found in the King James Version, it also details the fate of those who ignore these methods and warnings and follow after their own way.

Now, let us take a look at how the New International Versions destroys this method by substituting words that add absolutely no clarity, or sense for that matter, to these verses:

Isaiah 28:7–13, NIV:

(7) And these also stagger from wine and reel from beer: Priests and prophets stagger from beer and are befuddled with wine; they reel from beer, they stagger when seeing visions, they stumble when rendering decisions.

(8) All the tables are covered with vomit and there is not a spot without filth.

(9) "Who is it he is trying to teach? To whom is he explaining his message? To children weaned from their milk, to those just taken from the breast?

(10) For it is: Do and do, do and do, rule on rule, rule on rule; a little here, a little there."

(11) Very well then, with foreign lips and strange tongues God will speak to this people,

(12) to whom he said, "This is the resting place, let the weary rest"; and, "This is the place of repose"—but they would not listen.

> (13) So then, the word of the LORD to them will become: Do and do, do and do, rule on rule, rule on rule; a little here, a little there—so that they will go and fall backward, be injured and snared and captured.

Wine is also a symbol of doctrine, Jeremiah 51:7, Luke 5:37, and Revelation 14:8. When the NIV translators chose to translate the Hebrew word "shagah" as "stagger" rather than "erred," as did the KJV translators, they render the verse purely literal. The dual application of both verses 7 and 8 are lost, and a disconnect with the verses from Jeremiah, Luke, and Revelation above is the result. Verse 9 in the KJV connects 'milk' symbolically to doctrine as well. The NIV translators chose the alternative word "message" rather than "doctrine" as the KJV translators did. Although "message" may be an acceptable word replacement for the Hebrew word, "doctrine" as used in the KJV is better suited for the sentiments of the verse in English. A 'precept' is a commandment or direction given as a rule of action or conduct, an injunction as to moral conduct—a maxim. A 'line' is an indication of demarcation; boundary; or limit. This method of study or teaching simply put means: Precept upon precept is a thus saith the Lord (law) or principal or definitive statement in the Word of God. Line upon line is a supportive statement. It supports a precept and is dependent upon the context to be such. When the phrases *'precept upon precept'* and *'line upon line'* are replaced with *'do and do'* and *'rule on rule,'* verses 10 and 13, the method for rightly dividing the word of truth is destroyed rendering these verses ineffective for the dual meaning/application intended. By changing the wording, these verses are reduced to a single meaning and the spiritual significance is lost, as is the Biblical method for efficient Bible study.

> This very important duty enjoined upon the church by our Divine Lord is greatly neglected. It is not enough to merely read the Bible as we would read other books; for its precious truths are given in such a manner, "precept upon precept,

precept upon precept, line upon line, line upon line, here a little and there a little," that it is necessary to search the Sacred Volume. (March 2, 1852, JWe, *Advent Review and Sabbath Herald*, 100.2)

Subtle Deception

"Now the serpent was more **subtil** than any beast of the field which the LORD God had made. And he said unto the woman, Yea, hath God said, Ye shall not eat of every tree of the garden?" (Gen. 3:1, KJV).

To help clarify, here is a definition of "subtle": "sub·tle adj. sub·tler, sub·tlest. 1.a. So slight as to be difficult to detect or analyze; elusive. b. Not immediately obvious; abstruse. 2. Able to make fine distinctions. 3. Operating in a hidden, usually injurious way; 4. a. Characterized by skill or ingenuity; clever. b. Crafty or sly; devious. c. insidious.—sub'tle·ness n.—sub'tly adv" (*The American Heritage Dictionary*).

It is the design of the enemy of souls to destroy faith in the Protestant Bible. He has collaborated with various agencies throughout history to accomplish this end. It should not be surprising to anyone acquainted with his devices that he would continue his diabolical plan by enshrouding the true Word of God under a multiplicity of spurious bibles, the top seller among them being the NIV.

The very first example of Satan's subtlety in "re-writing" God's Word is found in Genesis 2:17 "But of the tree of the knowledge of good and evil, thou shalt not eat of it: for in the day that thou eatest thereof **thou shalt surely die.**" Satan twisted God's words in Genesis 3:4. "And the serpent said unto the woman, **Ye shall not surely die,**" where he changed the words from "thou shalt surely die" in Genesis 2:17 to "Ye shall not surely die" in Genesis 3:4. In Matthew 4:5–6 Satan tries to trick Jesus into sinning by perverting Psalms 91:12 and deliberately omitting part of verse 11: "Then the devil taketh him up into the holy city, and setteth him on a pinnacle of the temple, And saith unto him, If thou be the Son of God, cast thyself down: for it is written, He shall give his angels charge concerning thee: and in their hands they shall bear thee up, lest at any time thou dash thy foot against a stone." Verse 11 says: "For he shall give his angels charge over thee, to keep thee in all thy ways."

As you can see in the examples above how Satan replaced God's words with his own words or removed God's words altogether from Scripture is the same way he does it in the modern "bible" versions. The King James version aptly describe Satan in John 8:44—"Ye are of your father the devil, and the lusts of your father ye will do. He was a murderer from the beginning, and abode not in the truth, because there is no truth in him. When he speaketh a lie, he speaketh of his own: for he is a liar, and the father of it."

Missing Verses

Technically, there are seventeen missing verses in the Critical Greek Text if you count 1 John 5:7, which is partially in the body of most modern versions. Footnotes attempting to justify the exclusion of these verses do little more than give the illusion of the chapter having the same number of verses as the KJV. Westcott speaks of noting in the margin what "seemed likely or noticeable—after Griesbach's manner" in their Greek manuscript in a letter to Hort. See the quote under the caption "Writing to Hort September 29th:" on page 20. It's curious that the Critical Greek Text did exactly what Westcott suggested. The following is a list of those missing verses followed by another testimony of Jesus witness of their importance immediately after. For a clearer understanding of the Spirit of Prophecy quotes association with each missing verse, you may have to study the contextual placement of these scriptures in the Bible. For that, you will need an Authorized King James Version Bible and access to the Spirit of Prophecy books referenced.

Matthew 17:21: "Howbeit this kind goeth not out but by prayer and fasting."

> The words of Christ pointing to His death had brought sadness and doubt. And the selection of the three disciples to

accompany Jesus to the mountain had excited the jealousy of the nine. Instead of strengthening their faith by prayer and meditation on the words of Christ, they had been dwelling on their discouragements and personal grievances. In this state of darkness, they had undertaken the conflict with Satan.

In order to succeed in such a conflict they must come to the work in a different spirit. Their faith must be strengthened by fervent prayer and fasting, and humiliation of heart. They must be emptied of self, and be filled with the Spirit and power of God. Earnest, persevering supplication to God in faith—faith that leads to entire dependence upon God, and unreserved consecration to His work—can alone avail to bring men the Holy Spirit's aid in the battle against principalities and powers, the rulers of the darkness of this world, and wicked spirits in high places. (White, *Desire of Ages*, p. 431)

Matthew 18:11: "For the Son of man is come to save that which was lost."

Before Christ came to the world, his home was in the kingdom of glory, among beings that had never fallen. They loved him, and he might have stayed there and rejoiced in their love. But he did not do this. He left the royal courts, and went without the camp, bearing the reproach of sin. **He came to a world all marred and seared by the curse to save the lost sheep; and he gathered into his divine bosom all that would come to him.** He was a Man of sorrows and acquainted with grief. He trod the rugged path of self-denial himself, and so set us an example. This was the work of Christ for us. Had he not done this, we should have been left to perish without hope in God. ("Co-Laborers with Christ," *The Signs of the Times*, December 3, 1885, par. 2)

Matthew 23:14: "Woe unto you, scribes and Pharisees, hypocrites! For ye devour widows' houses, and for a pretence make long prayer: therefore ye shall receive the greater damnation."

> "Woe unto you, scribes and Pharisees, hypocrites! for ye devour widows' houses, and for a pretense make long prayer: therefore ye shall receive the greater damnation." The Pharisees had great influence with the people, and of this they took advantage to serve their own interests. They gained the confidence of pious widows, and then represented it as a duty for them to devote their property to religious purposes. Having secured control of their money, the wily schemers used it for their own benefit. To cover their dishonesty, they offered long prayers in public, and made a great show of piety. **This hypocrisy Christ declared would bring them the greater damnation. The same rebuke falls upon many in our day who make a high profession of piety**. Their lives are stained by selfishness and avarice, yet they throw over it all a garment of seeming purity, and thus for a time deceive their fellow men. But they cannot deceive God. He reads every purpose of the heart, and will judge every man according to his deeds." (White, *Desire of Ages*, p. 614.2; emphasis added)

Mark 7:16: "If any man have ears to hear, let him hear."

> The instruction received by those who listened to Jesus was to be communicated by them to others, and thus handed down to posterity. He also declared that there was nothing hidden that should not be manifested. Whatever was in the heart would sooner or later be revealed by the actions; and these would determine whether the seed sown had taken root in their minds and borne goodly fruit, or whether the thorns and brambles

had won the day. **He admonished them to hear and understand him**. To improve the blessed privileges then extended to them, would result in their own salvation and through them would benefit others. (White, *The Spirit of Prophecy*, Vol. 2, p. 243.1)

Mark 9:44: "Where their worm dieth not, and the fire is not quenched."
Mark 9:46: "Where their worm dieth not, and the fire is not quenched."

We read of chains of darkness for the transgressor of God's law. **We read of the worm that dieth not, and of the fire that is not quenched. Thus is represented the experience of every one who has permitted himself to be grafted into the stock of Satan, who has cherished sinful attributes.** When it is too late, he will see that sin is the transgression of God's law. He will realize that because of transgression, his soul is cut off from God, and that God's wrath abides on him. This is a fire unquenchable, and by it every unrepentant sinner will be destroyed. Satan strives constantly to lead men into sin, and he who is willing to be led, who refuses to forsake his sins, and despises forgiveness and grace, will suffer the result of his course. ("Christ and the Law," *Signs of the Times*, April 14, 1898, par. 13; emphasis added)

Mark 11:26: "But if ye do not forgive, neither will your Father which is in heaven forgive your trespasses."

"And when ye stand praying, forgive, if ye have aught against any: that your Father also which is in heaven may forgive you your trespasses. But if ye do not forgive, neither will your Father which is in heaven forgive your trespasses." **The law and the gospel declare this precept, and enforce this command**: "Therefore all things whatsoever ye would that men should do to you, do ye even so to them: for this is the law and the prophets." "Love worketh no ill to his neighbor: therefore love is the fulfilling of the law." ("Because He First Loved Us," *The Youth's Instructor*, January 13, 1898, par. 8; emphasis added)

Mark 15:28: "And the scripture was fulfilled, which saith, And he was numbered with the transgressors."

The thieves crucified with Jesus were placed "on either side one, and Jesus in the midst. This was done by the direction of the priests and rulers. Christ's position between the thieves was to indicate that He was the greatest criminal of the three. **Thus was fulfilled the scripture, "He was numbered with the transgressors." Isaiah 53:12.** But the full meaning of their act the priests did not see. As Jesus, crucified with the thieves, was placed "in the midst," so His cross was placed in the midst of a world lying in sin. And the words of pardon spoken to the penitent thief kindled a light that will shine to the earth's remotest bounds. (White, *Desire of Ages*, p. 751.4; emphasis added)

> *The Lord is coming in power and great glory. It will then be His work to make a complete separation between the righteous and the wicked.*

Luke 17:36: "Two men shall be in the field; the one shall be taken, and the other left."

The **Lord is coming in power and great glory. It will then be His work to make a complete separation between the righteous and the wicked.** But the oil cannot then be transferred to the vessels of those who have it not. Then shall be fulfilled the words of Christ, "Two women shall be grinding together; the one shall be taken, and the other left. Two men shall be in the field; the one shall be taken, and the other left." The righteous and the wicked are to be associated together in the work of life. But the Lord reads the character, He discerns who are obedient children, who respect and love His commandments. ("The Preparation Needed," *The Bible Echo*, May 4, 1896, par. 2)

Luke 23:17: "(For of necessity he must release one unto them at the feast.)"

It was customary at this feast to release some one prisoner whom the people might choose. This custom was of pagan invention; there was not a shadow of justice in it, but it was greatly prized by the Jews. The Roman authorities at this time held a prisoner named Barabbas, who was under sentence of death. This man had claimed to be the Messiah. He claimed authority to establish a different order of things, to set the world right.... Under cover of religious enthusiasm he was a hardened and desperate villain, bent on rebellion and cruelty. By giving the people a choice between this man and the innocent Saviour, Pilate thought to arouse them to a sense of justice. He hoped to gain their sympathy for Jesus in opposition to the priests and rulers. So, turning to the crowd, he said with great earnestness, "Whom will ye that I release unto you? Barabbas, or Jesus which is called Christ?" (White, *Desire of Ages*, p. 733.1)

John 5:4: "For an angel went down at a certain season into the pool, and troubled the water: whosoever then first after the troubling of the water stepped in was made whole of whatsoever disease he had."

"Now there is at Jerusalem by the sheep market a pool, which is called in the Hebrew tongue Bethesda, having five porches. In these lay a great multitude of impotent folk, of blind, halt, withered, waiting for the moving of the water. For an angel went down at a certain season into the pool, and troubled the water; whosoever then first after the troubling of the water stepped in was made whole of whatsoever disease he had."

Jesus did not hold himself aloof from the poor, the suffering, and sinful. His great heart of love went out in yearning tenderness for wretched objects who needed his help. **He was acquainted with the sufferers who had learned to look forward to the period when it was thought that the waters were agitated by a supernatural power.** Many suffering from different maladies visited the pool; but so great was the crowd at the appointed time, that they rushed forward, trampling under foot men, women, and children weaker than themselves. (White, *The Spirit of Prophecy*, Vol. 2, p. 156–157; emphasis added)

Acts 8:37: "And Philip said, If thou believest with all thine heart, thou mayest. And he answered and said, I believe that Jesus Christ is the Son of God."

In this instance we have an illustration of the care of God for his children. He called Philip from his successful ministry in Samaria, to cross the desert and go to Gaza to labor for a single inquiring soul. The promptness with which the eunuch accepted the gospel and acted upon its belief should be a lesson to us. God designs that we should be prompt in accepting and confessing Christ, prompt in obeying him, and in answering the call of duty. The eunuch was a man of good repute, and occupied a high and responsible position. **Through his conversion the gospel was carried to Ethiopia, and many there** accepted Christ, and came out from the darkness of heathenism into the clear light of Christianity. (White, *The Spirit of Prophecy*, Vol. 3, p.305.1; emphasis added)

Acts 15:34: "Notwhithstanding it pleased Silas to abide there still."

The broad and far-reaching decisions of the general council brought confidence into the ranks of the Gentile believers, and the cause of God prospered. In Antioch the church was favored with the presence of Judas and Silas, the special messengers who had returned with the apostles from the meeting in Jerusalem. **"Being prophets also themselves," Judas and Silas, "exhorted the brethren with many words, and confirmed them." These godly men tarried in Antioch for a time.** "Paul also and Barnabas continued in Antioch, teaching and preaching the word of the Lord, with many others also." (White, *The Acts of the Apostles*, p.197.2; emphasis added)

Acts 24:7: "But the chief captain Lysias come upon us, and with great violence took him away out of our hands."

That an apostate from Israel should presume to profane the temple at the very time when thousands had come there from all parts of the world to worship, excited the fiercest passions of the mob. "They took Paul, and drew him out of the temple: and forthwith the doors were shut."

"As they went about to kill him, tidings came unto the chief captain of the band, that all Jerusalem was in an uproar." **Claudius Lysias well knew the turbulent elements with which he had to deal, and he "immediately took soldiers and centurions, and ran down unto them: and when they saw the chief captain and the soldiers, they left beating of Paul."** Ignorant of the cause of the tumult, but seeing that the rage of the multitude was directed against Paul, the Roman captain concluded that he must be a certain Egyptian rebel of whom he had heard, who had thus far escaped capture. He therefore "took him, and commanded him to be bound with two chains; and demanded who he was, and what he had done." (White, *The Acts of the Apostles*, p.407.3; emphasis added)

Acts 28:29: "And when he had said these words, the Jews departed, and had great reasoning among themselves."

Some of Paul's hearers eagerly received the truth, but others stubbornly refused to be convinced. The testimony of the Scriptures was presented before them by one who was their equal in learning and their superior in mental power, and who had the special illumination of the Holy Spirit. They could not refute his arguments, but refused to accept his conclusions. **The prophecies which the rabbis themselves applied to Christ were a great annoyance to these opposing Jews; for the apostle showed that the fulfillment of these very prophecies required them to accept of Christ.** His humble entry into Jerusalem, his rejection by his own people, the treachery of Judas, the paltry sum paid for his betrayal, his death as a malefactor, even the bitter, stupefying draughts offered him in his dying agony, the lots cast upon his garments, his victory over death and the grave by the resurrection on the third day, his final exaltation on the right hand of God,—all these were in direct fulfillment of the words of the prophets. **But the more conclusive the arguments presented, the more determined were the Jews in their opposition.** Frenzied with malice, they reiterated their assertions that Jesus of Nazareth was a deceiver. (White, *Sketches from the Life of Paul*, p. 277.2; emphasis added)

Romans 16:24: "The grace of our Lord Jesus Christ be with you all. Amen."

> Though he was a prisoner, Paul was not discouraged. Instead, a note of triumph rings through the letters that he wrote from Rome to the churches. "Rejoice in the Lord alway," he wrote to the Philippians, "and again I say, Rejoice.... Be careful for nothing; but in everything by prayer and supplication with thanksgiving let your requests be made known unto God. And the peace of God, which passeth all understanding, shall keep your hearts and minds through Christ Jesus. Finally, brethren, whatsoever things are true, whatsoever things are honest, whatsoever things are just, whatsoever things are pure, whatsoever things are lovely, whatsoever things are of good report; if there be any virtue, and if there be any praise, think on these things."
>
> My God shall supply all your need according to His riches in glory by Christ Jesus.... **The grace of our Lord Jesus Christ be with you all.** (White, *The Acts of the Apostles*, p. 484; emphasis added)

1 John 5:7: "For there are three that bear record in heaven, the Father, the Word, and the Holy Ghost: and these three are one."

> Christ, our Mediator, and the Holy Spirit are constantly interceding in man's behalf, but the Spirit pleads not for us as does Christ, who presents His blood, shed from the foundation of the world; the Spirit works upon our hearts, drawing out prayers and penitence, praise and thanksgiving. The gratitude which flows from our lips is the result of the Spirit striking the cords of the soul in holy memories, awakening the music of the heart." (Ellen G. White Manuscript 50, 1900)

> I testify the things which I have seen, the things which I have heard, the things which my hands have handled of the Word of life. And this testimony I know to be of the Father and the Son. We have seen and do testify that the power of the Holy Ghost has accompanied the presentation of the truth, warning with pen and voice, and giving the messages in their order. To deny this work would be to deny the Holy Ghost, and would place us in that company who have departed from the faith, giving heed to seducing spirits. (White, *Selected Messages*, Vol. 2, p. 388.2)

Another subtle deception of modern versions is the attempt to mislead their readers to believe that missing verses are not missing at all, by referencing those missing verses in a footnote and maintaining the same number of verses as the KJV. Casual readers do not read footnotes, and even if they did, they are programed to see the missing verses as unnecessary for a correct understanding of Scripture. Of course, die-hard proponents of modern versions present various justifications for this practice. However, doesn't it make sense to boldly declare that these verses do not belong if one truly believes they do not? If the codices these versions come from are truly superior, there should be no reason to conceal the fact that those verses are not included, and chapters are consequently shorter. But those codices (Sinaiticus (Aleph) and Vaticanus, 'B') also contain books of the Apocrypha—again, it only makes reasonable sense that those apocryphal books should be included in the modern versions, if the "translators" of those versions truly believe those codices used to be superior to the Textus Receptus.

Still another subtle deception is the inclusion of these deleted verses in the body of some of the electronic Bibles (NIV84) while merely footnoting them in the body of the printed versions. It is much easier to compare versions with electronic bible applications than it would be with the printed volumes. Some applications contain multiple Bibles and the ability to compare them side by side. Although the missing verses are usually written with a lighter colored font, there is no explanation in the application as to why that is. Could the answer be that electronic Bibles like e-sword and *The Blue Letter Bible* make it too easy to compare them to the KJV? Those verses have been removed from the 2011 electronic edition of the NIV. They have been replaced by a footnote in some of the on-line electronic editions.

Changes and Deletions

A note in the margin of the NIV tells the reader that "[The earliest manuscripts and many other ancient witnesses do not have John 7:53–8:11.]". While these verses are included in the body of most modern versions, the NIV84 includes the note above in the body also. Could these verses be slated for removal as well, and made mention of as mere footnotes in future editions? Most Bible revisionists readily admit that Bible revision is never a finished work. The woman caught in adultery and brought to Jesus for judgment is the story presented in these verses. Below is what the Testimony of Jesus says about those scriptures:

> But in the early morning He returned to the temple; and as the people gathered about Him, He sat down and taught them.
>
> He was soon interrupted. A group of Pharisees and scribes approached Him, dragging with them a terror-stricken woman, whom with hard, eager voices they accused of having violated the seventh commandment. Pushing her into the presence of Jesus, they said, with a hypocritical display of respect, "Master, this woman was taken in adultery, in the very act. Now Moses in the law commanded us, that such should be stoned: but what sayest Thou?" (Verses 4, 5).
>
> Their pretended reverence veiled a deep-laid plot for His ruin. Should Jesus acquit the woman, He might be charged

with despising the law of Moses. Should He declare her worthy of death, He could be accused to the Romans as one who assumed authority belonging only to them. (White, *The Ministry of Healing*, p. 86–88)

The NIV says the same thing in the margin about Mark 16:9–20, Jesus' resurrection and ascension. Below is what the Testimony of Jesus says about those verses:

Through the gift of the Holy Spirit the disciples were to receive a marvelous power. Their testimony was to be confirmed by signs and wonders. Miracles would be wrought, not only by the apostles, but by those who received their message. Jesus said, "In My name shall they cast out devils; they shall speak with new tongues; they shall take up serpents; and if they drink any deadly thing, it shall not hurt them; they shall lay hands on the sick, and they shall recover." Mark 16:17, 18.

At that time poisoning was often practiced. Unscrupulous men did not hesitate to remove by this means those who stood in the way of their ambition. Jesus knew that the life of His disciples would thus be imperiled. Many would think it doing God service to put His witnesses to death. He therefore promised them protection from this danger. (White, *Desire of Ages*, p. 821)

Job 21:19–20

Job 21:19–20, KJV:
"God layeth up his iniquity for his children: he rewardeth him, and he shall know it. His eyes shall see his destruction, and he shall drink of the wrath of the Almighty."

Job 21:19–20, NIV:
"It is said, **'God stores up a man's punishment for his sons.'** Let him repay the man himself, so that he will know it! Let his own eyes see his destruction; let him drink of the wrath of the Almighty."

Job 21:19–20, NKJV:
"They say, **'God lays up one's iniquity for his children'**; Let Him recompense him, that he may know it. Let his eyes see his destruction, And let him drink of the wrath of the Almighty."

Here is another example of where the New King James Version also follow the error of the Nestle/Aland Greek text used by the New International and the other modern versions. Job 21:19 in the King James Version is obviously speaking of the children of those who hate God and raise their children accordingly. See Exodus 20:5 The erroneous rendering of these verses in modern versions distorts the very character of God. Verse 20 in the NKJV and the NIV even presume to correct God when they suggest that the man should be responsible for his sins rather than his children being held responsible. Ezekiel 18:20, KJV, says in no uncertain terms: "The soul that sinneth, it shall die. **The son shall not bear the iniquity of the father, neither shall the father bear the iniquity of the son:** the righteousness of the righteous shall be upon him, and the wickedness of the wicked shall be upon him."

There is a consistency in scripture text in the King James Bible that you will not find in the modern versions. Ezekiel 18:20 is also supported by Deuteronomy 24:16 "The fathers shall not be put to death for the children, neither shall the children be put to death for the fathers: every man shall be put to death for his own sin."

Job 21:30

After comparing Job 21:30 in the KJV with the rendering of it in the NIV, many people, need no more evidence for recognizing the diabolical nature of modern versions, as the NIV states the exact opposite of the KJV:

Job 21:30, KJV:
"That the **wicked is reserved** to the day of destruction? they shall be **brought forth to the day of wrath**."

Job 21:30, NIV:
"That the **evil man is spared** from the day of calamity, that he is **delivered from the day of wrath**?"

If the writings of Ellen White are not supported by modern versions, is it logical to believe that she would have endorsed them had they existed in her lifetime? There are many today that believe she would have. They site her occasional use of the RV and the ARV as their rationale for that belief. The statement below is obviously harmonious with the KJV rendering of Job 21:30. The wicked will most definitely not be spared from the day of judgment. Job is speaking to his three friends who were accusing him of sin as the reason for his predicament. See Job 21:27. His question to them in the first part of verse 30 is: "Don't you know the fate of the wicked as every passer by does" (author's paraphrase)? The second part of that verse is a statement of fact that the NIV and many other modern versions simply get wrong.

> At the general conference of believers in the present truth, held at Sutton, (Vt.) September, 1850, I was shown that the seven last plagues will be poured out after Jesus leaves the Sanctuary. Said the angel, **It is the wrath of God and the Lamb that causes the destruction or death of the wicked**. At the voice of God the saints will be mighty and terrible as an army with banners; but they will not then execute the judgment written. **The execution of the judgment will be at the close of the 1000 years**. (White, *A Sketch of the Christian Experience and Views of Ellen G. White*, p.33.1; emphasis added)

2 Peter 2:9

This unbiblical gospel of punishment before judgment is a theme throughout modern versions. The change in 2 Peter 2:9 is yet another example of this erroneous philosophy.

2 Peter 2:9, KJV:
"The Lord knoweth how to deliver the godly out of temptations, and to reserve the unjust unto the day of judgment **to be punished**:"

2 Peter 2:9, NIV84:
"If this is so, then the Lord knows how to rescue godly men from trials and to hold the unrighteous for the day of judgment, **while continuing their punishment**."

2 Peter 2:9, NKJV:
"Then the Lord knows how to deliver the godly out of temptations and to reserve the unjust **under punishment for the day of judgment**."

Mark 7:19

Mark 7:19, KJV:
"Because it entereth not into his heart, but into the belly, and goeth out into the draught, purging all meats?"

Mark 7:19, NIV:
"For it doesn't go into his heart but into his stomach, and then out of his body. **(In saying this, Jesus declared all foods clean.)**"

Mark 7:19, NKJV:
"Because it does not enter his heart but his stomach, and is eliminated, **thus purifying all foods?**"

Religious proponents for eating whatever one pleases to eat have tried for decades to make a scriptural case for disobeying God's health laws in the Old Testament scripture forbidding such practices. Translators of modern versions attempt to support this philosophy by adding the emboldened text to Mark 7:19. Following is the agreement of the testimony of Jesus with the KJV:

> To Peter, who had imbibed the teachings of the Pharisees, the words of Christ seemed new and strange. He said to Christ, "Declare unto us this parable. And Jesus said, Are ye also yet without understanding? Do not ye yet understand, that whatsoever entereth in at the mouth goeth into the belly, and is cast out into the draught? But those things which proceed out of the mouth come forth from the heart; and they defile the man. For out of the heart proceed evil thoughts, murders, adulteries, fornications, thefts, false witness, blasphemies; these are the things which defile a man; but to eat with unwashen hands defileth not a man." ("Ye Teach for Doctrine the Commandments of Men," *The Signs of the Times*, January 3, 1900, par. 10)

> *Many of the advocates of modern versions promote the idea that there have been no theological nor doctrinal differences resulting from the wording changes in modern versions. This author hopes that what the reader has read thus far proves the opposite true.*

Revelation 5:9–10

Many of the advocates of modern versions promote the idea that there have been no theological nor doctrinal differences resulting from the wording changes in modern versions. This author hopes that what the reader has read thus far proves the opposite true. Revelation 5:9 and 10, in particular, show the damage to doctrine done by modern versions.

Revelation 5:9–10, KJV:
"And they sung a new song, saying, Thou art worthy to take the book, and to open the seals thereof: for thou wast slain, and hast **redeemed us** to God by thy blood out of every kindred, and tongue, and people, and nation; And hast made **us** unto our God kings and priests: and **we** shall reign on the earth."

Revelation 5:9–10, NIV:
"And they sang a new song, saying: 'You are worthy to take the scroll and to open its seals, because you were slain, and with your blood you **purchased for God persons** from every tribe and language and people and nation. You have made **them** to be a kingdom and priests to serve our God, and **they** will reign on the earth.'"

Although we do not know beyond all doubt that the twenty-four elders are made up of that group resurrected with Christ (see Matt. 27:52–53), we can be sure that like them, the twenty-four elders were indeed redeemed from the earth as the King James version rightly says. Astute Bible students and historians like J.N. Loughborough, Uriah Smith, S.H. Haskell, and Ellen White understood that the twenty-four elders were, in fact, redeemed human beings from the earth.

> Holy angels will join in the song of the redeemed. Though they cannot sing from experimental knowledge, "**He hath washed us in His own blood, and redeemed us unto God**," yet they understand the great peril from which the people of God have been saved. Were they not sent to lift up for them a standard against the enemy? They can fully sympathize with the glowing ecstasy of those who have overcome by the blood of the Lamb and the word of their testimony (Letter 79, 1900). (White, *SDA Bible Commentary* Vol. 7, p. 922.8; emphasis added)

Revelation 14:6–7

Revelation 14:6–7, KJV:

"And I saw another angel fly in the midst of heaven, having the everlasting gospel to preach unto them that dwell on the earth, and to every nation, and kindred, and tongue, and people, Saying with a loud voice, Fear God, and give glory to him; for the hour of his judgment is come: and worship him that made heaven, and earth, and the sea, and the fountains of waters."

Revelation 14:6–7, NIV:

"Then I saw another angel flying in midair, and **he** had the eternal gospel to proclaim to those who live on the earth—to every nation, tribe, language and people. **He** said in a loud voice, 'Fear God and give him glory, because the hour of his judgment has come. Worship him who made the heavens, the earth, the sea and the springs of water.'"

By adding the word "he" referring to the angel in this text makes it appear as though the text is speaking of an actual angel as opposed to a symbol of God's people who are to proclaim this message. Hear what the testimony of Jesus has to say:

> This message is declared to be a part of the "everlasting gospel." The work of preaching the gospel has not been committed to angels, but has been entrusted to men. Holy angels have been employed in directing this work, they have in charge the great movements for the salvation of men; but the actual proclamation of the gospel is performed by the servants of Christ upon the earth. (White, *The Great Controversy* 1888 ed., p. 311.3)

The insertion of the word 'he' in Revelation 14:16 and 17 are not only one of the subtlest changes in the modern version but arguably one of the most diabolical. All who love and understand truth should be alarmed and outraged. Revelation, chapter 14, dubbed the three angels' messages, are at the heart of the gospel for these last days to a dying and deceived world. What may appear to be minor changes in the wording of a statement to the casual reader, when the totality of those changes is considered, can change the intended meaning of that statement. Remember what Hort said about what may appear to be "trifling alterations"— "taken together, they have often important bearings which few would think of at first."

Revelation 22:14

Revelation 22:14, KJV:
"Blessed are they **that do his commandments**, that they may have right to the tree of life, and may enter in through the gates into the city."

Revelation 22:14, NIV:
"Blessed are those **who wash their robes**, that they may have the right to the tree of life and may go through the gates into the city."

According to the NIV, it is not necessary to keep God's commandments as a requisite for entrance into heaven. A washed robe seems to be enough. Although there is great spiritual significance to the phrase 'washed in the blood,' notice the cunning and the crafty way the New International Version attempts to spiritualize away the necessity for keeping God's commandments. In Revelation 1:5 Jesus washes us of our sins in His blood. But, what does that statement mean? It means he died for us and paid the price for sin, which is the transgression of the law (1 John 3:4), or breaking His commandments. *'Washing robes'* may appear to be an interchangeable term for *'do his commandments'* to those who bring their KJV understanding to the reading of the NIV. However, it is a clever attempt at doing away with the necessity of being victorious over sin as a requirement for entrance into heaven for those who believe victory over sin is not possible. The KJV plainly says in Revelation 22:14 that those who do His commandments will have a right to the tree of life and entrance into the Holy City. Those who merely think they are keeping His commandments do not have that same right. A profession of righteousness does not mean true righteousness.

The NIV, as well as other modern versions, alter Revelation 1:5 by using the word "freed" in the place of "washed." By doing this the linking word washed to Revelation 22:14 is disconnected from a cleansing from sin. Equally as clever is the fact that no significant change was made in Revelation 7:14 in the modern versions. It says "... and have washed their robes, and made them white in the blood of the Lamb." just as the KJV does. Why, you ask—because it supports the supposition that somehow our sins can be washed away without actually doing the commandments of God and that we can have the right to heaven as a result, as stated in Revelation 22:14 of the NIV.

> The dim glory of the Jewish age has been succeeded by the brighter, clearer glory of the Christian age. But not once has Christ stated, that His coming destroyed the claims of God's law. On the contrary, in the very last message to His church, by way of Patmos, He pronounces a benediction upon those who keep His Father's law: "Blessed are they that do his commandments, that they may have right to the tree of life, and may enter in through the gates into the city." ("Christ and the Law," *Signs of the Times*, July 29, 1886)
>
> We must educate ourselves to talk faith, and prepare for the future life. What earnest efforts men make to obtain a lawful title to their land. They must have deeds that will stand the test of law. The possessor is never satisfied unless he is confident that there is no flaw in his title. O that men were as earnest to obtain a title to their heavenly possessions that would stand the test of law! The apostle exhorts the follower of Christ to give diligence to make his calling and election sure. There must be no error, no flaw in your claim to immortality. Says the Saviour, "Blessed are they that do His commandments, that they may

have right to the tree of life, and may enter in through the gates into the city." (White, "We Should Glorify God," *Review and Herald*, April 30, 1889)

Luke 2:14

Luke 2:14, KJV:
"Glory to God in the highest, and **on earth peace, good will toward men.**"

Luke 2:14, NIV:
"Glory to God in the highest, and **on earth peace to men on whom his favor rests.**"

When Isaiah foretold the birth of the Messiah, he ascribed to him the title, "Prince of peace." **When angels announced to the shepherds that Christ was born, they sung above the plains of Bethlehem, "Glory to God in the highest, and on earth peace, good will toward men."** [Luke 2:14.] There is a seeming contradiction between these prophetic declarations and the words of Christ, "I came not to send peace, but a sword." [Matthew 10:34.] But rightly understood, the two are in perfect harmony. The gospel is a message of peace. Christianity is a system, which, received and obeyed, would spread peace, harmony, and happiness throughout the earth. **The religion of Christ will unite in close brotherhood all who accept its teachings. It was the mission of Jesus to reconcile men to God, and thus to one another.** But the world at large are under the control of Satan, Christ's bitterest foe. The gospel presents to them principles of life which are wholly at variance with their habits and desires, and they rise in rebellion against it. They hate the purity which reveals and condemns their sins, and they persecute and destroy those who would urge upon them its just and holy claims. It is in this sense—because the exalted truths it brings, occasion hatred and strife—that the gospel is called a sword. (White, *The Great Controversy*, 1888 ed., p. 46.2; emphasis added)

I hope that the true nature of modern versions is becoming clearer to you, the reader. These Bibles are not only ecumenical but spiritualistic, esoteric, and even demonic. There are so-called initiates who believe that the peace of God rests on men especially favored by Him. This school of thought also gives way to philosophy or theory of predestination. The grace of God through Jesus Christ as heralded by the angels in Luke 2:14 is for every man, woman, and child of every age.

Mark 10:21

Mark 10:21, KJV:
"Then Jesus beholding him loved him, and said unto him, One thing thou lackest: go thy way, sell whatsoever thou hast, and give to the poor, and thou shalt have treasure in heaven: and come, **take up the cross**, and follow me."

Mark 10:21, NIV:
"Jesus looked at him and loved him. 'One thing you lack,' he said. 'Go, sell everything you have and give to the poor, and you will have treasure in heaven. Then come, follow me.'"

> God has spoken, and He means that man shall obey. He does not inquire if it is convenient for him to do so. The Lord of life and glory did not consult His convenience or pleasure when He left His station of high command to become a man of sorrows and acquainted with grief, accepting ignominy and death in order to deliver man from the consequence of his disobedience.

Jesus died, not to save man in his sins, but from his sins. Man is to leave the error of his ways, to follow the example of Christ, **to take up his cross and follow Him,** denying self, and obeying God at any cost. (White, *Counsels for the Church*, p. 269; emphasis added)

The cross is a symbol of crucifixion, and to take up one's cross is symbolic of dying daily to sin, the world, and its allurements. "The true source of wisdom and virtue and power is the cross of Calvary. Christ is the author and finisher of our faith. He says, 'Without me ye can do nothing'" ("Seek First the Kingdom of God," *Review and Herald*, February 7, 1893). To remove those words from the Bible is to remove a vital element of practical Christianity.

> *"The true source of wisdom and virtue and power is the cross of Calvary. Christ is the author and finisher of our faith. He says, 'Without me ye can do nothing.'"*

Perhaps an argument can be made for the use of synonyms and alternate wording of verses in modern Bible versions. No doubt some readers of this book will attempt to make that very argument to justify those changes. However, that argument is easily defeated if one inserts a synonym for a word that gives an obviously different connotation of the contexts of a Scripture. For example, 1 Timothy 3:16 of the KJV reads: "And without controversy great is the mystery of godliness: God was manifest in the flesh, justified in the Spirit, seen of angels, preached unto the Gentiles, believed on in the world, received up into glory." If one changed the word "manifest" in this verse for one of its synonyms such as the word "obvious," it is easy to see that the use of this word changes what the verse was attempting to convey. If a not so obvious synonym like the word "visible" were used to replace "manifest," the meaning of the verse is changed, but more subtly.

CHAPTER 5

In Spite of, Not Because of

> "The words of the Lord are pure words: as silver tried in a
> furnace of earth, purified seven times" (Ps.12:6, KJV).

In the face of the many injunctions in the authorized word of God forbidding the changing of the meaning of Scripture (i.e., Revelation 22:18, 19; 2 Corinthians 2:17 and 4:2), many believe that the Lord is actually not all that particular about it. Many sincere Christians promote the idea that God will save the sincere repentant sinner regardless of the Bible version he chooses to use. But is that true? Can a person comply with the requirements of God without knowing what those requirements are? Or is it possible that God can save us despite our choice of a Bible?

Have you ever wondered about the many statements made by the so-called biblical scholars that there are no doctrinal changes in the many Bibles on the market? Do not statements like that beg the question: if, there is no difference, why create them in the first place? If there are so many Bibles, and they all read differently, then which Bible is the real Word of God? Or are we to believe that what is different is, in all actuality, the same? Can you, the reader, see the resulting doubt of the truth of God's word that arises out of the conflicting words of modern Bible versions?

Some may be thinking at this point, surely Christ can still be found in these modern Bibles. And they would be right to a degree. A watered-down, impotent Christ can be found in these modern versions. A Christ whose divinity is difficult to prove, as you will see in Chapter 6: Is Jesus The Christ.

The predominant English Bible before 1881 was the Authorized King James Bible. The entire Protestant world understood the Authorized Bible to be the inerrant Word of God given by inspiration to fallible men. The first modern version, the Revised Version, appeared in 1881. By now we understand its dubious beginnings.

Diligent study of the Scripture bears out the fact that God's last day remnant people of prophecy would have the gift of the spirit of prophecy as testified in Revelation 12:17 and 19:10 (see chapter 7). Of course, these scriptures are grossly distorted in just about all modern versions thereby dislodging them from other linking verses throughout the Scriptures. Beliefs like the Investigative Judgment, the Heavenly Sanctuary, and Christian perfection have come under attack in many Protestant churches by some of its "scholars" because of modern Bible versions. As you can see from a sampling of scripture below that modern versions, do not support perfection of the saints. The NIV, being indicative of most modern versions, use synonyms and alternative wording that breaks the chain that links other supportive doctrinal texts using the same word.

Ezekiel 28:15, KJV:

"Thou wast **perfect** in thy ways from the day that thou wast created, till iniquity was found in thee."

Ezekiel 28:15, NIV:

"You were **blameless** in your ways from the day you were created till wickedness was found in you."

1 Peter 5:10, KJV:

"But the God of all grace, who hath called us unto his eternal glory by Christ Jesus, after that ye have suffered a while, make you **perfect**, stablish, strengthen, settle you."

1 Peter 5:10, NIV:

"And the God of all grace, who called you to his eternal glory in Christ, after you have suffered a little while, will himself restore you and make you **strong**, firm and steadfast."

The testimony of Jesus Christ contains the following statement in agreement with the King James Bible:

> So perfect is the character represented which men must have in order to be Christ's disciples that the infidel has said that it is not possible for any human being to attain unto it. But no less a standard must be presented by all who claim to be children of God. Infidels know not that celestial aid is provided for all who seek for it by faith. Every provision has been made in behalf of every soul who shall seek to be a partaker of the divine nature, and be complete in Jesus Christ. Every defect is to be discerned and cut away from the character with an unsparing decision. (Ellen G. White letter 117–1896 [November 3, 1896] par. 21), (White, *In Heavenly Places*, p. 201.2)

From the inception of the Seventh-day Adventist church, not one Seventh-day Adventist scholar or theologian has ever sat or was asked to sit on the myriad of Bible version committees starting with the Oxford Movement, in the mid-1800s, which insinuated a need to revise the Bible. Despite this fact, many SDA scholars, leaders, and theologians alike insist on the reliability of these spurious versions. Of course, when a statement like this one is made the response often is: "there were no Seventh-day Adventists on the committee that compiled the 1611 Authorized Version either." The short answer to that retort obviously is that the SDA church did not exist at that time. However, true Seventh-day Adventism is Protestantism, and in that respect, it had a hand in the compilation of the King James Bible. Although this book will not delve into all of what true Protestantism is, if you continue reading you will discover that true Protestantism does not allow for a Bible that promotes the same apostasy the early Protestant reformers resisted.

I hope that by now you, the reader, understand that all the doctrine and theology of the Protestant churches were forged without the existence of modern versions. That these versions with all their word additions and deletions demote our biblical understanding to cultish nonsense. Yet, there are those among us who insist one can be saved without having the benefit of the truth at their disposal.

"Watch and pray, that ye enter not into temptation" (Matt. 26:41, KJV). What are we watching and praying for? Satan's devices, prophetic fulfillment, conditions leading to the National Sunday Law. If Satan is evil as the Word describes him, seeking whom he may devour, why should we want to believe that he would not seek to counterfeit God's Word to accomplish this end? Has he not done this very thing in the past? Following are a few quotes from the Spirit of Prophecy showing just how important the Bible is to us, emphasizing why the enemy of souls wants to destroy it:

> The Bible is second to no other book; it is without a rival. A knowledge and acceptance of its teachings will impart vigor and health of mind; a comprehension of its teachings requires the student to grasp the knowledge of God's infinite will. The Word of God teaches men and women how to become the sons and daughters of God. No other book, no other study can equal this; the principles it instills, like the power and nature of its Author, are omnipotent. It is capable of imparting the highest education to which the mortal mind can attain. (Ellen G. White letter 64-1909.3 [April 5, 1909])

It is not safe for us to turn from the Holy Scriptures, with only a casual reading of their sacred pages. Dig deep for truth as you would for hidden treasure. Every page of God's word is illuminated by the light of the Sun of righteousness, and the utterances of prophets and apostles are full of freshness and power. Rein the mind up to the high task that has been set before it, and study with determined interest, that you may understand divine truth. Those who do this, will be surprised to find to what the mind can attain. As we endeavor to use our talents as God would have us, they strengthen and increase, until we can grasp sacred and elevated themes. As long as we are content with little things, and fail to study to show ourselves approved unto God, workmen that need not to be ashamed, rightly dividing the word of truth, we shall meet with great loss. The blessed book of God assures us that we may grow spiritually, that there is no need of becoming religious dwarfs, by indolence disqualifying ourselves to do the very work that is waiting to be done. By placing ourselves in right relation with the source of all light, we may accomplish great things for God and humanity. ("Words to the Young," *The Youth Instructor*, June 29, 1893, par. 6)

> *Dig deep for truth as you would for hidden treasure. Every page of God's word is illuminated by the light of the Sun of righteousness.*

The Bible is our guide in the safe paths that lead to eternal life. God has inspired men to write that which will present the truth to us, which will attract, and which, if practised, will enable the receiver to obtain moral power to rank among the most highly educated minds. The minds of all who make the word of God their study will enlarge. Far more than any other study, this is of a nature to increase the powers of comprehension, and endow every faculty with new vigor. It brings the mind in contact with broad, ennobling principles of truth. It brings us into close connection with all heaven, imparting wisdom, and knowledge, and understanding. ("Search the Scriptures," *The Youth's Instructor*, October 13, 1898, par. 7)

As a means for intellectual training, the Bible is more effective than any other book, or all other books combined. The greatness of its themes, the dignified simplicity of its utterances, the beauty of its imagery, quicken and uplift the thoughts as nothing else can. No other study can impart such mental power as does the effort to grasp the stupendous truths of revelation. The mind thus brought in contact with the thoughts of the Infinite can not but expand and strengthen.

And even greater is the power of the Bible in the development of the spiritual nature. Man, created for fellowship with God, can only in such fellowship find his real life and development. Created to find in God his highest joy, he can find in nothing else that which can quiet the cravings of the heart, or satisfy the hunger and thirst of the soul. He who with sincere and teachable spirit studies God's Word, seeking to comprehend its truths, will be brought into touch with its Author, and, except by his own choice, there is no limit to the possibilities of his development. ("Our Great Treasure-House," *Signs of the Times*, September 19, 1906, par. 5–6)

"And if we have minds of limited capacity, by diligently searching the word of God we may become mighty in the Scriptures, and may explain them to others." ("Search the Scriptures," *The Review and Herald*, April 3, 1888, par. 3)

If these words are indeed true, it makes sense that our great adversary would do everything in his power to make God's Word void. How absurd then is it to think that because God convicts a person of his/her need while using one of the modern Bible versions, that that is His (God's) ideal method of saving an individual. Though many prisoners convert while in jail, most know that prison was not God's chosen method to reach them. Yes, God convicts souls of their need despite their circumstances, not because of them.

> Satan failed in his temptations to Christ in the wilderness. The plan of salvation has been carried out. The dear price has been paid for man's redemption. And now Satan seeks to tear away the foundation of the Christian's hope and turn the minds of men into such a channel that they may not be benefited or saved by the great sacrifice offered. He leads fallen man, through his "all deceivableness of unrighteousness," to believe that he can do very well without an atonement, that he need not depend upon a crucified and risen Saviour, that man's own merits will entitle him to God's favor. **And then he destroys man's confidence in the Bible, well knowing that if he succeeds here, and faith in the detector which places a mark upon himself is destroyed, he is safe.** He fastens upon minds the delusion that there is no personal devil, and those who believe this make no effort to resist and war against that which they think does not exist. Thus poor, blind mortals finally adopt the maxim, "Whatever is, is right." They acknowledge no rule to measure their course. (White, *Testimonies for the Church*, Vol. 1 p. 294.2; emphasis added)

CHAPTER 6

Is Jesus The Christ?

"Who is a liar but he that denieth that Jesus is the Christ?
He is antichrist, that denieth the Father and the Son"
(1 John 2:22 KJV).

It is important to reiterate the point that the changing of the wording in the Bible is not to be taken lightly. As mentioned in previous chapters, there are fearful warnings in the word of God forbidding any from distorting its meaning.

Jesus said in the Gospel of John 5:39 of the King James Bible: "Search the scriptures; for in them ye think ye have eternal life: and they are they which testify of me." If modern Bible versions consistently diminish the divinity of Christ, His creatorship, His atonement for us, and His bodily resurrection, it is not possible for them to testify of Jesus Christ, and cannot possibly lead you to eternal life. The rationalization that God can save through the use of modern versions places God in league with the devil. The correct rationale is that God can save in spite of the use of modern versions.

Isaiah 14:12

From a casual reading of Isaiah 14:12 in the NIV the reader more than likely will not notice the name Lucifer has been removed. Generally, it is only noticed when that verse is compared with that of the KJV, and not any of the other modern Bible versions.

Isaiah 14:12, KJV:
"How art thou fallen from heaven, **O Lucifer, son of the morning!** how art thou cut down to the ground, which didst weaken the nations!"

Isaiah 14:12, NIV:
"How you have fallen from heaven, **morning star, son of the dawn!** You have been cast down to the earth, you who once laid low the nations!"

By removing the name Lucifer as the NIV and the other modern versions have done, and presenting him as the "morning star" as opposed to the "son of the morning" as stated in the KJV, Christ is now depicted as the fallen angel just as He is in Gnostic writings. When you also consider Revelation 22:16 which reads basically the same in the modern translations as it does in the KJV, "I Jesus have sent mine angel to testify unto you these things in the churches. I am the root and the offspring of David, *and* **the bright and morning star**," Jesus calls Himself the bright and morning star. But this is inconsistent with Isaiah 14:12 in the modern translations unless, true to Gnosticism, Lucifer becomes the Christ of Revelation 22:16 and Christ become the fallen angel of Isaiah 14:12.

The name "Lucifer" only appears in Isaiah 14:12 of the KJV, the removal of that name from this verse effectively disconnects Lucifer and Satan as the same individual in all modern versions except for the NKJV. Nearly all Bible texts mentioning Satan speaks of him as evil. Therefore, those who worship Lucifer can detach the attributes of Satan from Lucifer and have biblical support for doing so.

However, the King James Bible once again corroborates the testimony of Jesus found in *Desire of Ages*, page 52:

> The Shekinah had departed from the sanctuary, but in the Child of Bethlehem was veiled the glory before which angels bow. This unconscious babe was the promised seed, to whom the first altar at the gate of Eden pointed. This was Shiloh, the peace giver. It was He who declared Himself to Moses as the I AM. It was He who in the pillar of cloud and of fire had been the guide of Israel. This was He whom seers had long foretold. He was the Desire of all nations, the Root and the Offspring of David, and the **Bright and Morning Star**. The name of that helpless little babe, inscribed in the roll of Israel, declaring Him our brother, was the hope of fallen humanity. The child for whom the redemption money had been paid was He who was to pay the ransom for the sins of the whole world. He was the true "high priest over the house of God," the head of "an unchangeable priesthood," the intercessor at "the right hand of the Majesty on high." Hebrews 10:21; 7:24; 1:3. (White, *Desire of Ages*, p. 55; emphasis added)

Philippians 2:7–8

In chapter one, it was shown that Westcott and Hort did not believe that Jesus Christ is God. Woven into their translation, and the theme of virtually all modern translations is the removal of the God divesting Himself of His Glory and becoming a man as seen in Philippians 2:7–8.

Philippians 2:7–8, KJV:

"But made himself of no reputation, and took upon him the **form** of a servant, and **was made in the likeness of men**: (8) And being found in **fashion** as a man, he humbled himself, and became obedient unto death, even the death of the cross."

Philippians 2:7–8, NIV:
"Rather, he made himself nothing, taking the very **nature** of a servant, **being made in human likeness**. And being found in **appearance** as a man, he humbled himself and became obedient to death—even death on a cross!"

Philippians 2:7–8, NKJV:
"But made Himself of no reputation, taking the **form** of a bondservant, and **coming in the likeness of men**. (8) And being found in **appearance** as a man, He humbled Himself and became obedient to the point of death, even the death of the cross."

According to Genesis 2:7 "And the LORD God formed man of the dust of the ground, and breathed into his nostrils …" To form something means to bring together parts or combine to create—or make. Jesus took to Himself the tangible characteristics of a man, He became verily a man. Likewise, Jesus took upon Himself the form of a man/servant and was made in the likeness of men. If He took only the mere *nature* (used here as an idiom means the basic or inherent features of a man) and *appearance* (the way that someone or something looks), it could be justifiably said that although Jesus looked like a man, he was not actually a man like as we are. A mannequin or a robot can have the inherent features of a man, that does not make it a man. To replace the word *fashion* (to make into a particular or the required form) with one of its synonyms—*appearance*—is to change the meaning of the text itself. We are told in 1 John 4:3, KJV, the spirit of antichrist would do this very thing. "And every spirit that confesseth not that Jesus Christ is come in the flesh is not of God: and this is that spirit of antichrist, whereof ye have heard that it should come; and even now already is it in the world."

Lucifer had said, "I will exalt my throne above the stars of God: ... I will be like the most High" (Isa. 14:13–14). But Christ, "**being in the form of God**, thought it not robbery to be equal with God: But made himself of no reputation, and took upon him the form of a servant, and was made in the likeness of men." (Phil. 2:6–7)

This was a voluntary sacrifice. Jesus might have remained at the Father's side. He might have retained the glory of heaven, and the homage of the angels. But He chose to give back the scepter into the Father's hands, and to step down from the throne of the universe, that He might bring light to the benighted, and life to the perishing. (White, *Desire of Ages*, p. 22)

1 Timothy 3:16

When 1 Timothy 3:16 of the Authorized Version is compared to the NIV and other modern versions it is not very difficult to see another example of the Godhood of Jesus Christ diminished.

1 Timothy 3:16, KJV:
"And without controversy great is the mystery of godliness: **God** was **manifest** in the **flesh, justified in the Spirit**, seen of angels, preached unto the Gentiles, believed on in the world, received up into glory."

1 Timothy 3:16, NIV:
"Beyond all question, the mystery from which true godliness springs is great: **He appeared** in the flesh, was **vindicated by the Spirit**, was seen by angels, was preached among the nations, was believed on in the world, was taken up in glory."

Paul is referring to Jesus Christ when he calls Him God in this text. By replacing "*God*" with the pronoun "*He*" the reference to Jesus is still in place. However, the reference to Jesus Christ as God has been removed. *Manifest* means plain, open, clearly visible, or obvious to the understanding; apparent; not obscure or difficult to be seen or understood. *Appear* means to come into sight; become visible or noticeable. The use of the word *manifest* in the KJV denotes that He (God) actually came in the flesh as a man and not merely *appeared* in a body while actually being something other than a man.

Justified in the Spirit is a reference to Christ before the incarnation. To justify is to declare or make righteous in the sight of God. To vindicate is to show that someone or something that has been criticized or doubted is correct, true, or reasonable. Jesus Christ was declared righteous and declared God (in the Spirit) before the incarnation. To be vindicated by the Spirit is a concept entirely foreign to the word of God. Justify and vindicate, although similar in meaning, communicate a subtle but different understanding of the verse. Replacing one word for the other changes the meaning and understanding of who Christ really is.

Malachi 4:2

Malachi 4:2 is another reference to Jesus Christ as the Day Star or Sun of righteousness. That is why the word Sun is capitalized in this verse in the King James Bible. The NIV and many of the modern versions render this verse as the literal sun, hence the words "healing in its rays" in the Today's New International Version (TNIV) and the 2011 edition of the NIV. Growing up as calves of the stall is a reference to us attaining the stature we had in Adam before the fall (See Ellen White's *Spiritual Gifts*, Volume 4a, page 119.2).

Malachi 4:2, KJV:

"But unto you that fear my name shall the Sun of righteousness arise with healing in **his wings**; and ye shall go forth, and **grow up as calves of the stall**."

Malachi 4:2, NIV84:
"But for you who revere my name, the sun of righteousness will rise with healing in **its rays**. And you will go out and **frolic like well-fed calves**."

> But when he ascended up on high, and led a multitude of captives, escorted by the heavenly host, and was received in through the gates of the city, with angelic songs of triumph and rejoicing, I beheld with admiration and wonder, that he possessed the same exalted stature that he had before he came into the world to die for man. Said the angel, God, who wrought so great a miracle as to make Christ flesh to dwell among men, and will with his almighty power lift up fallen, degenerate, and dwarfed man, and after they are redeemed from the earth, make them **"grow up as calves of the stall,"** could in his infinite power return to his dear Son his own exalted stature, which was his before he left Heaven, and humbled himself as a man, and submitted to the death of the cross. (White, Spiritual Gifts, Vol. 4a, p. 119; emphasis added)

There were two famous people, commonly referred to in Christendom as "Church Fathers," named Clement and Origen. Both were professors at the metaphysical college of Alexandria in the early third century of the Christian era, and both were concerned to present Christianity in a way that would be acceptable to Christians and pagans alike.

To this end, Origen set about corrupting the Holy Scriptures and in this he was so successful that later Bishop Eusebius made use of his work while translating a Bible that would help Constantine unite pagan Rome with Christianity.

The historian John Mosheim tells how Clement played his part in popularising Christianity by blending Gnosticism with Christian truth, producing a form of Christianity that was veiled by and shrouded under the precepts of [Greek] philosophy (Mosheim Commentaries, cent 2, Vol. 1, p. 341).

In furtherance of this objective, Clement invented a system of allegorising and misapplying Scripture. One pertinent example is found in his misuse of Malachi 4:2 ... in 1985 the Church brought out a new hymnal. For the first time, the General Conference bestowed its imprimatur on a hymnbook by naming it the "Seventh-day Adventist Hymnal." It felt confident in lending the Church's good name to this hymnal because it had appointed a Church Hymnal Committee to examine carefully each hymn for scriptural and doctrinal soundness (Introduction to Hymnal, p. 6). We are also told that, *To the left [of each hymn] is found a Bible reference if the hymn is based on a specific passage [of Scripture].*

Such statements are indeed assuring. The General Conference has taken admirable precautions to protect our spiritual wellbeing. Well, that's how it should be. But alas! Such is not the case.

Let us turn to Hymn No 403.
"Let us break bread together on our knees ...
Let us drink wine together on our knees
When I fall on my knees with my face to the **rising sun**
O Lord have mercy on me."

Surely there has been some mistake here! This is not the way Adventists partake of the emblems. Perhaps the inclusion of this strange hymn was an unfortunate oversight? But what's this at the top left hand corner? A Scriptural reference? Malachi 4:2!

So the inclusion of this hymn is not a mistake. Its inclusion is justified by a specific passage of Scripture. By getting down on our knees with our face to the rising sun we are somehow honouring Jesus Christ—the Sun of righteousness! Then why not give Him even greater honour by worshipping Him on the day of the sun? In so doing we would also be wonderfully celebrating the day of our Lord's victory - His resurrection." (Meyers, *The Dismantling of Adventism*, p. 137–139)

Daniel 3:25

Modern Bible versions reduce Jesus Christ in importance to that of any other false god:

> *The Hebrew captives filling positions of trust in Babylon had in life and character represented before him the truth. When asked for a reason of their faith, they had given it without hesitation.*

Daniel 3:25, KJV:
"He answered and said, Lo, I see four men loose, walking in the midst of the fire, and they have no hurt; and the form of the fourth is **like the Son of God.**"

Daniel 3:25, NIV:
"He said, 'Look! I see four men walking around in the fire, unbound and unharmed, and the fourth looks **like a son of the gods.**'"

"... Lo, I see four men loose, walking in the midst of the fire, and they have no hurt; and the form of the fourth is like the Son of God."

How did that heathen king know what the Son of God was like? The Hebrew captives filling positions of trust in Babylon had in life and character represented before him the truth. When asked for a reason of their faith, they had given it without hesitation. Plainly and simply they had presented the principles of righteousness, thus teaching those around them of the God whom they worshiped. **They had told of Christ, the Redeemer to come; and in the form of the fourth in the midst of the fire the king recognized the Son of God.** (White, *Prophets and Kings*, p. 509–510)

Ephesians 3:9

Jesus Christ as our Creator and Redeemer has been substantially diminished in the NIV and the NKJV as He has in the Jehovah's Witness NWT (New World Translation). See also John 1:1–3 and Hebrews 1:2. By changing the word *world* to *age* the connotation of an actual creation of the literal world is changed into an intangible time period.

Ephesians 3:9, KJV:
"And to make all men see what is the fellowship of the mystery, **which from the beginning of the world** hath been hid in God, **who created all things by Jesus Christ.**"

Ephesians 3:9, NIV:
"And to make plain to everyone the administration of this mystery, **which for ages past** was kept hidden in God, who created all things."

Ephesians 3:9, NKJV:
"And to make all see what is the fellowship of the mystery, **which from the beginning of the ages** has been hidden in God **who created all things through Jesus Christ.**"

Luke 9:55–56

The context of the following verses is Christ reproving the ill-tempered brothers (John and James) who wanted to destroy a city because Jesus was not received well by its inhabitants. In Christ's reproof, He reiterated His mission to save that which was lost, Matthew 18:11 (omitted from modern versions). The NIV, as does most modern versions, remove the wording necessary for correctly understanding the role and who Jesus is; for the Roman Catholic theology which paints Jesus as a tyrant requiring Mary as a mediator between Christ and man.

Luke 9:55–56, KJV:
"But he turned, and rebuked them, **and said, Ye know not what manner of spirit ye are of. For the Son of man is not come to destroy men's lives, but to save them**. And they went to another village."

Luke 9:55–56, NIV:
"But Jesus turned and rebuked them. Then he and his disciples went to another village."

Matthew 8:2

Where the word "worshipped" is used in the KJV referring to the worship of Jesus Christ, the NIV changes it to "knelt." See also Matthew 9:18, 15:25, 18:26, Mark 5:6, and Mark 15:19. These changes were first done in the Jehovah's Witnesses New World Translation (NWT). The NWT also used the same corrupt sources as the NIV and other modern versions. That is why it's not surprising that these verses are rendered the same way. What is surprising, however, is the fact that the "Protestant" community rejects the NWT, yet accepts all of the other modern versions.

Matthew 8:2, KJV:
"And, behold, there came a leper and **worshipped** him, saying, Lord, if thou wilt, thou canst make me clean."

Matthew 8:2, NIV:
"A man with leprosy came and **knelt** before him and said, 'Lord, if you are willing, you can make me clean.'"

Mark 1:40–41

Are we really to believe Jesus Christ is the tyrant the modern versions try to portray Him as? Look how He is portrayed simply by substituting the word *indignant* in place of *compassion*. Compassion is a noun meaning sympathetic pity and concern for the sufferings or misfortunes of others. Its synonyms are *pity, sympathy, empathy, fellow feeling, care, concern, solicitude, sensitivity, warmth, love, tenderness, mercy, leniency, tolerance, kindness, humanity, charity*. All the attributes of Jesus. Indignant is an adjective meaning feeling or showing anger or annoyance at what is perceived as unfair treatment. Its synonyms are *aggrieved, resentful, affronted, disgruntled, displeased, cross, angry, mad, annoyed, offended, exasperated, irritated, chagrined*.

Mark 1:40–41, KJV:

"And there came a leper to him, beseeching him, and kneeling down to him, and saying unto him, If thou wilt, thou canst make me clean. And Jesus, moved with **compassion**, put forth his hand, and touched him, and saith unto him, I will; be thou clean."

Mark 1:40–41, NIV 2011:

"A man with leprosy came to him and begged him on his knees, 'If you are willing, you can make me clean.' Jesus was **indignant**. He reached out his hand and touched the man. 'I am willing,' he said. 'Be clean!'"

Who but Satan or his agents would use indignant to describe our Lord and Savior? Listen to how He is described by the Spirit of Prophecy:

> When our weakness becomes strength in Christ, we shall not be craving for amusement. Then holidays, that are considered so indispensable, will not be used simply for the gratification of self; but they will be turned into occasions in which you can bless and enlighten souls. When weary, Jesus sought for a place of rest in the desert; but the people had had a taste of the

heavenly manna, and they came out to him in large companies. In all their human woe and suffering and distress, they sought his retreat, and there was no rest for the Son of God. **His heart was moved with compassion**; for they were as sheep without a shepherd, and his great heart of love was touched with the feeling of their infirmities, and he taught them concerning the kingdom of heaven. **Jesus was never cold and unapproachable.** ("Christ and His Righteousness," *Bible Echo and Signs of the Times*, June 15, 1892, par. 5; emphasis added)

Matthew 17:17

Another example of the portrayal of an indignant Jesus in the modern versions can be found in Matthew 17:17 of the NIV. Here the word *be* is replaced with *stay*, and the words *suffer you* are replaced with the words *put up with you*. The NIV, by replacing these words, alters the meaning of the verse to imply Jesus is weary of serving the people when He was actually implying that He had a limited physical time with them to get His message across.

Matthew 17:17, KJV:
"Then Jesus answered and said, O faithless and perverse generation, how long shall I **be** with you? how long shall I **suffer you**? bring him hither to me."

Matthew 17:17, NIV:
"'O unbelieving and perverse generation,' Jesus replied, 'how long shall I **stay** with you? How long shall I **put up with you**? Bring the boy here to me.'"

Genesis 22:8

Genesis 22:8, KJV:
"And Abraham said, My son, **God will provide himself a lamb** for a burnt offering: so they went both of them together.'

Genesis 22:8, NIV:

"Abraham answered, '**God himself will provide the lamb** for the burnt offering, my son.' And the two of them went on together."

Genesis 22:8, NKJV:

"And Abraham said, 'My son, **God will provide for Himself the lamb** for a burnt offering.' So the two of them went together."

The NIV as well as the other modern translations by changing the wording alter the meaning of this verse as well as the prophecy of Christ becoming the very lamb mentioned here. Note how the spirit of prophecy deals with the prophetic aspect of this verse:

> Upon Mount Moriah, Abraham had heard the question of his son, "My father, ... where is the lamb for a burnt offering?" The father answered, "My son, God will provide Himself a lamb for a burnt offering." Genesis 22:7, 8. And in the ram divinely provided in the place of Isaac, Abraham saw a symbol of Him who was to die for the sins of men. The Holy Spirit through Isaiah, taking up the illustration, prophesied of the Saviour, "He is brought as a lamb to the slaughter," "and the Lord hath laid on Him the iniquity of us all" (Isaiah 53:7, 6). (White, *Desire of Ages*, p. 112)

Proverbs 8:22–30

Prov. 8:22–30, KJV:

> The LORD **possessed me in the beginning of his way**, before his works of old. **I was set up from everlasting**, from the beginning, or ever the earth was. When there were no depths, **I was brought** forth; when there were no fountains abounding with water. Before the mountains were settled, before the hills was **I brought forth**; While as yet he had not made the earth, nor the fields, nor the highest part of the dust of the world. When

he prepared the heavens, **I was there**: when he set a compass upon the face of the depth: When he established the clouds above: when he strengthened the fountains of the deep: When he gave to the sea his decree, that the waters should not pass his commandment: Then I was by him, **as one brought up with him**: and I was daily his delight, rejoicing always before him.

Prov. 8:22–30, NIV:

The LORD brought me forth as the first of his works, before his deeds of old; **I was formed long ages ago**, at the very beginning, when the world came to be. When there were no watery depths, **I was given birth**, when there were no springs overflowing with water; before the mountains were settled in place, before the hills, **I was given birth**, before he made the world or its fields or any of the dust of the earth. I was there when he set the heavens in place, when he marked out the horizon on the face of the deep, when he established the clouds above and fixed securely the fountains of the deep, when he gave the sea its boundary so the waters would not overstep his command, and when he marked out the foundations of the earth. Then **I was constantly at his side.** I was filled with delight day after day, rejoicing always in his presence.

Prov. 8:30, NKJV:

"Then **I was beside Him as a master craftsman**; And I was daily His delight, Rejoicing always before Him.'

"And every spirit that confesseth not that Jesus Christ is come in the flesh is not of God: and this is that spirit of antichrist, whereof ye have heard that it should come; and even now already is it in the world" (1 John 4:3 KJV). Modern versions, in verses like Proverbs 8:22–30, deny that God (Jesus Christ) has come in the flesh. They subtly promote the idea that He is a created being. This is the spirit of antichrist thereby placing modern versions squarely in the antichrist camp.

The Sovereign of the universe was not alone in His work of beneficence. He had an associate—a co-worker who could appreciate His purposes, and could share His joy in giving happiness to created beings. "In the beginning was the Word, and the Word was with God, and the Word was God. The same was in the beginning with God." John 1:1, 2. Christ, the Word, the only begotten of God, was one with the eternal Father—one in nature, in character, in purpose—the only being that could enter into all the counsels and purposes of God. "His name shall be called Wonderful, Counselor, The mighty God, The everlasting Father, The Prince of Peace." Isaiah 9:6. His "goings forth have been from of old, from everlasting." Micah 5:2. And the Son of God declares concerning Himself: **"The Lord possessed Me in the beginning of His way, before His works of old. I was set up from everlasting.... When He appointed the foundations of the earth: then I was by Him, as one brought up with Him: and I was daily His delight, rejoicing always before Him."** Proverbs 8:22–30. (White, *Patriarch and Prophets*, p. 34)

Micah 5:2

Micah 5:2, KJV:
"But thou, Bethlehem Ephratah, though thou be little among the thousands of Judah, yet out of thee shall he come forth unto me that is to be ruler in Israel; **whose goings forth have been from of old, from everlasting**."

Micah 5:2, NIV:
"But you, Bethlehem Ephrathah, though you are small among the clans of Judah, out of you will come for me one who will be ruler over Israel, **whose origins are from of old, from ancient times**."

Does Jesus have an origin or was He without beginning or end as His Father is? According to many verses in the modern versions, He does, and that is the day He was created. The Spirit of Prophecy agrees with the KJV, "and the spirit of the prophets are subject to the prophets" (1 Corinthians 14:32, KJV).

> "His name shall be called Immanuel, ... God with us." "The light of the knowledge of the glory of God" is seen "in the face of Jesus Christ." **From the days of eternity the Lord Jesus Christ was one with the Father;** He was "the image of God," the image of His greatness and majesty, "the outshining of His glory." It was to manifest this glory that He came to our world. To this sin-darkened earth He came to reveal the light of God's love,—to be "God with us." Therefore it was prophesied of Him, "His name shall be called Immanuel." (White, *Desire of Ages*, p. 19.1)

There is a methodical changing of words throughout modern so-called Bible versions that systematically alter verses, doctrine, and prophecy as a result. In this section, we primarily focused on how Jesus Christ's Godhood is under attack. However, as you continue to study this modern Bible version phenomenon, by comparing scripture that prophesies Christ as the true God/man, you will undoubtedly uncover many more distortions of this nature. The scriptures presented here should be more than sufficient to place modern Bible versions under a thick cloud of suspicion. If you are using a Bible that diminishes Jesus as God, malign His character, and distort His mission; you are using a Bible that cannot lead you to eternal life.

CHAPTER 7

The Mark of the Beast

"And he shall speak great words against the most High, and shall wear out the saints of the most High, and think to change times and laws: and they shall be given into his hand until a time and times and the dividing of time" (Dan. 7:25, KJV).

The observance of Sunday, the first day of the week, in the place of the seventh-day Sabbath as commanded by God in the fourth commandment will become the mark of the beast when state law decrees it. The scope of this writing does not lend itself to a detailed study of the evidence that identifies the Roman Catholic Church as the beast power mentioned in the Bible whose dreaded "mark'" we are admonished not to take. For a detailed study on that subject, please read chapter 13 of the book of Revelation in the King James Bible and chapter 25, "God's Law Immutable" of *The Great Controversy*, by Ellen G. White. It makes sense, however, that to understand what the mark of the beast is, the identity of the beast must be understood.

As the sign of the authority of the Catholic Church, papist writers cite "the very act of changing the Sabbath into Sunday, which Protestants allow of; ... because by keeping Sunday, they acknowledge the church's power to ordain feasts, and to command them under sin."—Henry Tuberville, An Abridgment of the Christian Doctrine, page 58. What then is the change of the Sabbath, but the sign, or mark, of the authority of the Roman Church—"the mark of the beast"?

The Roman Church has not relinquished her claim to supremacy; and when the world and the Protestant churches accept a sabbath of her creating, while they reject the Bible Sabbath, they virtually [in all practicality] admit this assumption. They may claim the authority of tradition and of the Fathers for the change; but in so doing they ignore the very principle which separates them from Rome—that "the Bible, and the Bible only, is the religion of Protestants." The papist can see that they are deceiving themselves, willingly closing their eyes to the facts in the case. As the movement for Sunday enforcement gains favor, he rejoices, feeling assured that it will eventually bring the whole Protestant world under the banner of Rome. (White, *The Great Controversy*, p. 448)

Romanists declare that "the observance of Sunday by the Protestants is an homage they pay, in spite of themselves, to the authority of the [Catholic] Church."—Mgr. Segur, *Plain Talk About the Protestantism of Today*, page 213. The enforcement

> *The observance of Sunday, the first day of the week, in the place of the seventh-day Sabbath as commanded by God in the fourth commandment will become the mark of the beast when state law decrees it.*

of Sundaykeeping on the part of Protestant churches is an enforcement of the worship of the papacy—of the beast. Those who, understanding the claims of the fourth commandment, choose to observe the false instead of the true Sabbath are thereby paying homage to that power by which alone it is commanded. But in the very act of enforcing a religious duty by secular power, the churches would themselves form an image to the beast; hence the enforcement of Sundaykeeping in the United States would be an enforcement of the worship of the beast and his image. (White, *The Great Controversy*, p. 448)

There are numerous publications and other sources where the Roman Catholic Church identifies herself as changing the Sabbath day from the seventh day to the first day of the week. She claims this change to be a mark or sign of her ecclesiastical authority to declare feast and holy days. Following are a sampling of a few of the Roman Catholic church's claims for Sunday observance:

Letter from C.F. Thomas, Chancellor of Cardinal Gibbons on October 28, 1895:

> Of course the Catholic Church claims that the change was her act ... And the act is a MARK of her ecclesiastical power and authority in religious matters. (http://1ref.us/nn, accessed June 26, 2018)

John A. O'Brien, *The Faith of Millions: the Credentials of the Catholic Religion Revised Edition* (Our Sunday Visitor Publishing, 1974, pp. 400–401):

> But since Saturday, not Sunday, is specified in the Bible, isn't it curious that non-Catholics, who claim to take their religion directly from the Bible and not from the Church, observe Sunday instead of Saturday? Yes, of course, it is inconsistent; but

this change was made about fifteen centuries before Protestantism was born, and by that time the custom was universally observed. They have continued the custom even though it rests upon the authority of the Catholic Church and not upon an explicit text in the Bible. That observance remains as a reminder of the Mother Church from which the non-Catholic sects broke away—like a boy running away from home but still carrying in his pocket a picture of his mother or a lock of her hair. (http://1ref.us/ns, accessed June 26, 2017)

Notice what Ellen White says regarding this power claimed by the Catholic Church:

> When Sunday observance shall be enforced by law, and the world shall be enlightened concerning the obligation of the true Sabbath, then whoever shall transgress the command of God, to obey a precept which has no higher authority than that of Rome, will thereby honor popery above God. He is paying homage to Rome, and to the power which enforces the institution ordained by Rome. He is worshiping the beast and his image. As men then reject the institution which God has declared to be the sign of His authority, and honor in its stead that which Rome has chosen as the token of her supremacy, they will thereby accept the sign of allegiance to Rome,—"the mark of the beast." And it is not until the issue is thus plainly set before the people, and they are brought to choose between the commandments of God and the commandments of men, that those who continue in transgression will receive "the mark of the beast." (White, *The Great Controversy*, 1888, p. 449)

The change of the Sabbath is the sign or mark of the authority of the Romish church. Those who, understanding the claims of the fourth commandment, choose to observe the false Sabbath in the place of the true, are thereby paying homage to that power by which alone it is commanded. The mark of the beast is the papal Sabbath, which has been accepted by the world in the place of the day of God's appointment.

But no one has yet received the mark of the beast. The testing time has not yet come. There are true Christians in every church, not excepting the Roman Catholic communion. None are condemned until they have had the light and have seen the obligation of the fourth commandment. But when the decree shall go forth enforcing the counterfeit Sabbath, and the loud cry of the third angel shall warn men against the worship of the beast and his image, the line will be clearly drawn between the false and the true. Then those who still continue in transgression will receive the mark of the beast.

With rapid steps we are approaching this period. When Protestant churches shall unite with the secular power to sustain a false religion, for opposing which their ancestors endured the fiercest persecution, then will the papal Sabbath be enforced by the combined authority of church and state. There will be a national apostasy, which will end only in national ruin. (Ellen G. White, manuscript 51, 1899)

Modern Bible versions alter the wording to give evidence to a supposed tenuous or changeable character of the Lord's seventh-day Sabbath. Following are a few examples of these alterations:

Exodus 20:8–11

Exodus 20:8–11, KJV:

Remember the sabbath day, **to** keep it holy. Six days shalt thou labour, and do all thy work: But the seventh day is **the** sabbath **of** the LORD thy God: in it thou shalt not do any work, thou, nor thy son, nor thy daughter, thy manservant, nor thy maidservant, nor thy cattle, nor thy stranger that is within thy gates: For in six days the LORD made heaven and earth, the sea, and all that in them is, **and** rested the seventh day: **wherefore** the LORD blessed the sabbath day, and hallowed it.

Exodus 20:8–11, NIV:

Remember the Sabbath day **by** keeping it holy. Six days you shall labor and do all your work, but the seventh day is **a** sabbath **to** the LORD your God. On it you shall not do any work, neither you, nor your son or daughter, nor your male or female servant, nor your animals, nor any foreigner residing in your towns. For in six days the LORD made the heavens and the earth, the sea, and all that is in them, **but** he rested on the seventh day. **Therefore** the LORD blessed the Sabbath day and made it holy

Only by a correct understanding of the Genesis account of creation do the reasons for the subtle changes in the wording of the above scripture become obvious to the astute Bible student. Remembering the Sabbath of creation week denotes the creation of the seventh day of rest commemorating the completion of creation in six literal days. God declared the seventh day of creation week holy, rendering it impossible to keep any other day holy since God only, and not a man have the power to make anything holy. Replacing the word *'to'* with *'by'* in verse 8 attempts to lead the reader to think mankind can choose a day of his preference and keep it holy thereby causing it to be *'a'* Sabbath. However, it is only Roman Catholic dogma that claims a church has the power to make holy days.

By substituting the word *'the'* (definite article) for the word *'a'* (indefinite article) the significance of the seventh-day Sabbath as God's holy day for worshiping Him as the creator has been removed and replaced with whichever day one chooses as a Sabbath. The word *'of,'* as in "*Sabbath of the Lord,"* is a preposition introducing the noun 'Lord' as the one to whom the Sabbath belongs. While the word *'to'* is an adverb indicating the position of someone or something. By replacing the phrase *"Sabbath of the Lord"* with *"Sabbath to the Lord"* modern versions remove Christ as Lord of the Sabbath and leads the reader to believe that if he dedicates the day of his own choosing to God, it becomes an acceptable form of worship to Him. The definite article *"the"* describes an unmistakable time and the word *"of"* denotes ownership.

In addition to the six days of creation, God created a seventh day in which nothing was created by Him. Instead, He used it for rest, adoration, and reflection. Verse 11 of the KJV says *"and rested the seventh day: wherefore the LORD blessed the sabbath day, and hallowed it."* The use of the word *and* denotes the connection between God's rest and His creation. *Wherefore* or because he rested, answers the question why He hallowed the seventh day. The use of the word *but* in the modern versions causes a disconnect between God's rest and His creation. And replacing the word *wherefore* with *therefore* removes the reason for making the day holy and demotes it to the mere consequence of God resting on it.

These subtle changes either give assurance to those who want to believe that the seventh-day Sabbath can be changed to another day, or cause doubt in the minds of those who once believed that the seventh day is the Sabbath. Either way, the counter-reformation has somewhat to celebrate, and the ecumenical movement takes a giant step forward.

Exodus 31:15–16

Exodus 31:15–16, KJV:

"Six days may work be done; but in the seventh is **the** sabbath of rest, holy to the LORD: whosoever doeth any work in the sabbath day, he shall surely be put to death. Wherefore the children of Israel shall **keep** the sabbath, to **observe** the sabbath throughout their generations, for a **perpetual** covenant."

Exodus 31:15–16, NIV:

"For six days work is to be done, but the seventh day is **a** day of sabbath rest, holy to the LORD. Whoever does any work on the Sabbath day is to be put to death. The Israelites are to **observe** the Sabbath, **celebrating** it for the generations to come as a **lasting** covenant."

Again, we see the replacement of the definite article *'the'* being replaced with *'a'* in the NIV giving the reader the false impression that God did not create a specific day of rest. The NIV also replaces the word *'keep'* with *'observe'* and *'observe'* with *'celebrating'* in verse 16. Obviously, these three words have entirely different meanings, and this scripture in the NIV has an entirely different meaning than that of the KJV. The NIV says one can *observe* the Sabbath without actually *keeping* it while *celebrating* it without actually *observing* it. It is entirely up to you. The Sabbath is not perpetual, lasting forever according to the NIV, but merely *lasting*—a relative term.

Exodus 20:4–6

Exodus 20:4–6, KJV:

Thou shalt not make unto thee **any graven image**, or any likeness of any thing that is in heaven above, or that is in the earth beneath, or that is in the water under the earth. Thou shalt not bow down thyself to them, nor serve them: for I the LORD thy God am a jealous God, **visiting the iniquity of the fathers** upon the children unto the third and fourth generation of them that hate me; **And shewing mercy unto thousands** of them that love me, and keep my commandments.

Exodus 20:4–6, NIV:

You shall not make for yourself an image in the form of anything in heaven above or on the earth beneath or in the waters below. You shall not bow down to them or worship them; for I, the LORD your God, am a jealous God, **punishing the children for the sin of the fathers** to the third and fourth generation of those who hate me, **but showing love to a thousand generations** of those who love me and keep my commandments.

Roman Catholic theology punishes the children for the sins of the fathers. That is why a bad child can cause the anguish of a parent in purgatory. By using the word '*but*' rather than '*and*,' verse 6, gives the intended impression that God being a tyrant according to verse 5 of the NIV can still show love to a thousand generations. According to Ezekiel 18:20 in the KJV, children are never punished for the sins of the parents. However, Ezekiel 18:20 is also corrupted in the NIV as well.

The Roman Catholic church also removed the second commandment in their catechism, which instructs us not to bow down nor worship images. Therefore, there is no reckoning of image worship as sin in Catholicism. Image worship is an intrinsic part of their worship, so you can see the reason for altering this verse in the modern ecumenical Bibles. The Roman Catholic church also split the tenth commandment into two parts making it appear there are still ten, when there are only nine. A similar trick is also done in modern versions when a verse is removed and replaced by a reference to a footnote giving the appearance that the chapter contains the same amount of verses.

The following is grounded in the authenticity of the King James Bible:

> The Israelites had been specially charged not to lose sight of the commandments of God, in obedience to which they would find strength and blessing. "Take heed to thyself, and keep thy soul diligently," had been the word of the Lord to them through Moses, "lest thou forget the things which thine eyes have seen, and lest they depart from thy heart all the days of thy life: but teach them thy sons, and thy sons' sons." [Deut. 4:9.] The awe-inspiring scenes connected with the giving of the law at Sinai

were never to be forgotten. Plain and decided were the warnings that had been given Israel against the idolatrous customs prevailing among the neighboring nations. "Take ye ... good heed unto yourselves," was the counsel given; **"lest ye corrupt yourselves, and make you a graven image, the similitude of any figure,"** "and lest thou lift up thine eyes unto heaven, and when thou seest the sun, and the moon, and the stars, even all the host of heaven, shouldest be driven to worship them, and serve them, which the Lord thy God hath divided unto all nations under the whole heaven." **"Take heed unto yourselves, lest ye forget the covenant of the Lord your God, which He made with you, and make you a graven image, or the likeness of anything, which the Lord thy God hath forbidden thee."** Verses 15, 16, 19, 23. (White, *Prophets and Kings*, p. 294; emphasis added.)

Mark 2:25–28

Mark 2:25–28, KJV:

And he said unto them, Have ye never read what David did, when he had need, and was an hungered, he, and they that were with him? How he went into the house of God in the days of Abiathar the high priest, and did eat the shewbread, which is not lawful to eat but for the priests, and gave also to them which were with him? And he said unto them, The sabbath was made for man, and not man for the sabbath: **Therefore** the Son of man is Lord **also** of the Sabbath.

Mark 2:25–28, NIV:

He answered, "Have you never read what David did when he and his companions were hungry and in need? In the days of Abiathar the high priest, he entered the house of God and ate the consecrated bread, which is lawful only for priests to eat. And he also gave some to his companions." Then he said to them, "The Sabbath was made for man, not man for the Sabbath. **So** the Son of Man is Lord **even** of the Sabbath."

According to the Spirit of Prophecy:

> If it was right for David to satisfy his hunger by eating of the bread that had been set apart to a holy use, then it was right for the disciples to supply their need by plucking the grain upon the sacred hours of the Sabbath. Again, the priests in the temple performed greater labor on the Sabbath than upon other days. The same labor in secular business would be sinful; but the work of the priests was in the service of God. They were performing those rites that pointed to the redeeming power of Christ, and their labor was in harmony with the object of the Sabbath. But now Christ Himself had come. The disciples, in doing the work of Christ, were engaged in God's service, and that which was necessary for the accomplishment of this work it was right to do on the Sabbath day.
>
> *The object of God's work in this world is the redemption of man; therefore that which is necessary to be done on the Sabbath in the accomplishment of this work is in accord with the Sabbath law.*
>
> Christ would teach His disciples and His enemies that the service of God is first of all. The object of God's work in this world is the redemption of man; therefore that which is necessary to be done on the Sabbath in the accomplishment of this work is in accord with the Sabbath law. Jesus then crowned His argument by declaring Himself the "Lord of the Sabbath,"— One above all question and above all law. This infinite Judge acquits the disciples of blame, appealing to the very statutes they are accused of violating.

Jesus did not let the matter pass without administering a rebuke to His enemies. He declared that in their blindness they had mistaken the object of the Sabbath. He said, "If ye had known what this meaneth, I will have mercy, and not sacrifice, ye would not have condemned the guiltless." Matthew 12:7. Their many heartless rites could not supply the lack of that truthful integrity and tender love which will ever characterize the true worshiper of God.

Again Christ reiterated the truth that the sacrifices were in themselves of no value. They were a means, and not an end. Their object was to direct men to the Saviour, and thus to bring them into harmony with God. It is the service of love that God values. When this is lacking, the mere round of ceremony is an offense to Him. So with the Sabbath. It was designed to bring men into communion with God; but when the mind was absorbed with wearisome rites, the object of the Sabbath was thwarted. Its mere outward observance was a mockery. (White, *Desire of Ages*, p. 286.1)

The Jews understood that it was right for David to eat the bread set aside for a holy use because God deemed it so. However, they resisted Jesus permitting His disciples to do likewise. The extremely subtle change in wording: *Therefore* to *so* and *also* to *even* removes Christ's authority to justify His disciples. Just as God authorized David and his men to eat the showbread, Jesus authorized His disciples who were doing the Lord's business to eat the corn as they walked through the fields. Christ is sovereign over all things including the Sabbath day as indicated by using the words *therefore* and *also* in verse 28. *Therefore* is an adverb and is used to denote the consequence of something. To use *so*, a less precise word, in place of *therefore* demonstrates to this author that the NIV revisionist had a clear understanding of the preciseness of the wording used by the KJV translators. By replacing the word *also*, which means in addition to, with *even,* used to emphasize something surprising or extreme, Christ as the

Lord of the Sabbath is presented as merely a novel idea in the modern versions.

Acts 13:42

Acts 13:42, KJV:
"And when the **Jews** were gone out of the synagogue, the Gentiles besought that these words might be preached to them the next sabbath."

Acts 13:42, NIV:
"As **Paul and Barnabas** were leaving the synagogue, the people invited them to speak further about these things on the next Sabbath."

Another subtle trick of the enemy is to create biblical support for a Sabbath day change from the seventh day of the week to the first day, as done here in Acts 13:42 of the NIV. By replacing *Jews* with *Paul and Barnabas*, the modern Bible version revisionist are now able to show biblical support for a Jewish and a Christian Sabbath. For those who want to believe that, this verse appears to support Sunday as the Christian Sabbath.

Gentiles were deemed unclean by the Jews, so they were not allowed to worship inside the synagogues with them. Apparently, they could hear the message preached because they asked that it be preached to them the following Sabbath. Dispensational Christians believe the Sabbath was changed after Christ's resurrection. Therefore, it is not a far-fetched notion to see how the change in this verse fits the dispensational beliefs of some Christians.

Revelation 12:17 and 19:10

Revelation 12:17, KJV:
"And the dragon was wroth with the woman, and went to make war with the **remnant of her seed**, which keep the **commandments** of God, and **have** the testimony **of** Jesus **Christ**."

Revelation 12:17, NIV:
"Then the dragon was enraged at the woman and went off to wage war against the **rest of her offspring**—those who keep God's **commands** and **hold fast** their testimony **about** Jesus."

Revelation 19:10, KJV:
"And I fell at his feet to worship him. And he said unto me, See thou do it not: I am thy fellowservant, and of thy brethren that **have the testimony** of Jesus: worship God: for **the testimony of Jesus is the spirit of prophecy**."

Revelation 19:10, NIV:
"At this I fell at his feet to worship him. But he said to me, 'Don't do that! I am a fellow servant with you and with your brothers and sisters who **hold to the testimony** of Jesus. Worship God! For it is **the Spirit of prophecy who bears testimony to Jesus**.'"

Here we see another attempt of modern revisionists trying to divert attention away from God's law and the testimony of Jesus in Revelation 12:17 of the modern Bible versions. Notice how modern versions, in this case, the NIV, divert the attention of the reader from the *"remnant of her seed,"* God's people, to what it calls the *"rest of her offspring."* The remnant, God's last day church, is never to be confused with the mere offspring of Abraham. Only those of Abraham's offspring who keep the commandments of God and have the testimony of Jesus Christ are the remnant of her seed. *Seed* is another one of those words that connect different scriptures together throughout the Bible giving a broader understanding of God's Word. Remove those linking words, and you remove pivotal understanding of the plan of salvation. Below are examples of verses containing the linking word *seed*:

Genesis 3:15, KJV:
"And I will put enmity between thee and the woman, and between thy **seed** and her seed; it shall bruise thy head, and thou shalt bruise his heel."

Genesis 12:7, KJV:
'And the LORD appeared unto Abram, and said, Unto thy **seed** will I give this land: and there builded he an altar unto the LORD, who appeared unto him."

Galatians 3:16, KJV:
"Now to Abraham and his **seed** were the promises made. He saith not, And to seeds, as of many; but as of one, And to thy seed, which is Christ."

Galatians 3:16 shows that the seed is Christ, Revelation 12:17 above shows that the seed is His church. Both scriptures are correct and build upon one another. The seed is Jesus and He bruises the head of the serpent. The seed is also His people, and they overcame him by the blood of the Lamb, and by the word of their testimony, Revelation 12:11. Romans 16:20 also reiterates that the person of Jesus Christ bruises the head of the serpent through His people: "And the God of peace shall bruise Satan under your feet shortly. The grace of our Lord Jesus Christ *be* with you. Amen."

Compare also the words "keep the commandments of God," referencing God's ten commandment laws in the KJV version of Revelation 12:17 and the NIV's "God's commands" having no direct relation to the ten commandment laws. The necessity to keep God's ten commandments, of which the fourth is the mark or sign of His authority, is diminished in modern versions. By subtly removing God's ten commandments from this verse as the NIV does, the commandment to keep the seventh day Sabbath is also made void, opening a way for the acceptance of the spurious Sabbath—which is the mark of the beast.

Those who keep the commandments of God in Revelation 12:17 are also said to "**have** the testimony **of** Jesus **Christ**" in the KJV. However, the NIV says they "**hold fast** their testimony **about** Jesus." The significance of this change in modern versions is not readily apparent without the definition of the testimony of Jesus Christ supplied by Revelation 19:10 of the KJV. The testimony of Jesus Christ is the spirit of prophecy, a definition conspicuously changed in the NIV and most other modern translations.

The question is why? And the answer is that Satan will and has gone to great lengths to obscure God's last-day church (remnant) from the world. He doesn't want any to know that keeping God's commandments is required, that God has a last-day remnant church that keeps His commandments and has the gift as well as the understanding of prophecy just as Revelation 12:17 says.

The King James Version Bible supports the testimony of Jesus quoted below:

> "And the dragon was wroth with the woman, and went to make war with the remnant of her seed, which keep the commandments of God, and have the testimony of Jesus Christ." This prophecy points out clearly that the remnant church will acknowledge God in His law and will have the prophetic gift. Obedience to the law of God, and the spirit of prophecy has always distinguished the true people of God, and the test is usually given on present manifestations.
>
> In Jeremiah's day the people had no question about the message of Moses, Elijah, or Elisha, but they did question and put aside the message sent of God to Jeremiah until its force and power was wasted and there was no remedy but for God to carry them away into captivity.
>
> Likewise in the days of Christ the people had learned that Jeremiah's message was true, and they persuaded themselves to believe that if they had lived in the days of their fathers they would have accepted his message, but at the same time they were rejecting Christ's message, of whom all the prophets had written.
>
> As the third angel's message arose in the world, which is to reveal the law of God to the church in its fullness and power, the prophetic gift was also immediately restored. This gift has acted a very prominent part in the development and carrying forward of this message. (White, *Loma Linda Messages*, p. 33)

Revelation 9:4

Revelation 9:4, KJV:
"And it was commanded them that they should not hurt the grass of the earth, neither any green thing, neither any tree; but only those men which have not the seal of God **in** their foreheads."

Revelation 9:4, NIV:
"They were told not to harm the grass of the earth or any plant or tree, but only those people who did not have the seal of God **on** their foreheads."

Revelation 9:4, NKJV:
"They were commanded not to harm the grass of the earth, or any green thing, or any tree, but only those men who do not have the seal of God **on** their foreheads."

> "The seal of God's law is found in the fourth commandment. This only, of all the ten, brings to view both the name and the title of the Lawgiver. It declares him to be the Creator of the heavens and the earth, and thus shows his claim to reverence and worship above all others. Aside from this precept, there is nothing in the decalogue to show by whose authority the law is given. When the Sabbath was changed by the papal power, the seal was taken from the law. The disciples of Jesus are called upon to restore it, by exalting the Sabbath of the fourth commandment to its rightful position as the Creator's memorial and the sign of his authority." (White, *Spirit of Prophecy*, Vol. 4, p. 284)

The outward sign of the seal of God is obedience to the fourth commandment, which requires the keeping of the seventh-day Sabbath. Being sealed in the forehead means belief in and the keeping of all God's commandments. To change the wording of Revelation 9:4, 13:16, 14:1, 9, 22:4

to make the seal appear as an outward sign, is to give those who do not want to believe the truth a scriptural reference for believing the mark of the beast is a tattoo or a barcode of some kind.

Revelation 13:16–18 and 15:1–2

Revelation 13:16–18, KJV:

And he causeth all, both small and great, rich and poor, free and bond, to receive a mark **in** their right hand, or **in** their foreheads: And that no man might buy or sell, save he that had the mark, **or** the name of the beast, **or** the number of his name. **Here** is wisdom. Let him that hath **understanding** count the number of the beast: for it is the number of a man; and his number is Six hundred threescore and six.

Revelation 13:16–18, NIV:

It also forced all people, great and small, rich and poor, free and slave, to receive a mark **on** their right hands or **on** their foreheads, so that they could not buy or sell unless they had **the mark, which is the name of the beast or the number of its name. This calls for** wisdom. Let the person who has **insight** calculate the number of the beast, for it is the number of a man. That number is 666.

According to the KJV, there are three criteria for being able to buy or sell at the time the mark of the beast is given: 1) that you have the mark of the beast, 2) the name of the beast, or 3) the number of his name. According to the NIV, there is only one requirement, and that is to have the mark itself. The name and number only define the mark and are synonymous with it, not separate and distinct from it. The rendering of this verse in the NIV not only make it impossible for obedience to a law requiring Sunday worship to be the mark of the beast, because National Sunday Law is not the name of the beast, but it also makes it impossible to identify the beast as the Roman Catholic church.

> The beast with lamb-like horns commands "all, both small and great, rich and poor, free and bond, to receive a mark in their right hand, or in their foreheads; and that no man might buy or sell, save he that had the mark, or the name of the beast, or the number of his name." [Revelation 13:16, 17.] This is the mark concerning which the third angel utters his warning. It is the mark of the first beast, or the papacy, and is therefore to be sought among the distinguishing characteristics of that power. The prophet Daniel declared that the Roman Church, symbolized by the little horn, was to think to change times and laws, [Daniel 7:25.] while Paul styled it the man of sin, [2 Thessalonians 2:3, 4.] who was to exalt himself above God. Only by changing God's law could the papacy exalt itself above God; whoever should understandingly keep the law as thus changed would be giving supreme honor to that power by which the change was made. Such an act of obedience to papal laws would be a mark of allegiance to the pope in the place of God. (White, *The Spirit of Prophecy*, Vol. 4, p. 279)

Insight is the act or result of apprehending the inner nature of things or of seeing intuitively. Understanding is to have a mental grasp, to have comprehension. As if the words *understanding* and *insight* did not have obvious different connotations, the definitions are included above just to show that the difference in the uses of the words renders a different meaning of the verse itself. The calling for wisdom and the presence (here) of wisdom further alter the meaning of the verse. As you can see from the verses below, it appears the NIV translators are deliberately trying to change the meaning of these verses.

Revelation 15:1-2, KJV:

"And I saw another sign in heaven, great and marvellous, seven angels having the seven last plagues; **for in them is filled up the wrath of God**. And I saw as it were a sea of glass mingled with fire: **and them that had gotten the victory over the beast, and over his image, and over his mark,** *and* **over the number of his name**, stand on the sea of glass, having the harps of God."

Revelation 15:1-2, NIV:

"I saw in heaven another great and marvelous sign: seven angels with the seven last plagues—**last, because with them God's wrath is completed**. And I saw what looked like a sea of glass glowing with fire and, standing beside the sea, **those who had been victorious over the beast and his image and over the number of his name**. They held harps given them by God."

An image to the first beast would be an organization, or second beast, functioning on much the same principles as the first beast. Among the principles by which the first beast operated was the use of the secular arm to support religious institutions. In imitation, the second beast will repudiate its principles of freedom. The church will prevail upon the state to enforce its dogmas. State and church will unite, and the result will be the loss of religious liberty and the persecution of dissenting minorities. (Compare with Rev. 13:12; see *The Great Controversy*, pp. 443–448.)

> Mark. Gr. *charagma*, "an impress," "a stamp," "a mark." This is evidently some badge of loyalty to the beast, some special feature that denotes that the one displaying such a mark worships the first beast, whose deadly wound was healed (v. 8). Adventist interpreters understand this mark to be not a literal brand but some sign of allegiance that identifies the bearer as loyal to the power represented by the beast. The controversy at that time will center on the law of God, and particularly on the fourth command (see on ch. 14:12). Hence, Sunday observance

will constitute such a sign, but not until the time when the beast's power will be revived and Sunday observance in place of Sabbath observance becomes law....

It should be noted that the beast has already been conclusively identified (see on vs. 1–10). The number provides confirmatory evidence of this. Since the early days of Christianity there has been much discussion as to the significance of 666. One of the earliest to write on the subject was Irenaeus (c. A.D. 130–c. A.D. 202). He identified the beast as the Antichrist and believed that the numerical values of the letters of his name would add up to 666. He suggested the name Teitan, a name sometimes accounted divine, as having great probability. He also suggested, but as much less probable, the name Lateinos, this being the name of the last kingdom of the four seen by Daniel. At the same time he warned that "it is therefore more certain, and less hazardous, to await the fulfillment of the prophecy, than to be making surmises, and casting about for any names that may present themselves, inasmuch as many names can be found possessing the number mentioned" (*Against Heresies* v. 30. 3; *ANF*, vol. 1, p. 559).

> *Sunday observance will constitute such a sign, but not until the time when the beast's power will be revived and Sunday observance in place of Sabbath observance becomes law.*

Since Irenaeus' day 666 has been applied to many names. The number alone cannot identify the beast since numerous names can add up to 666. However, inasmuch as the beast has already been identified, the number 666 must have a relationship to this power. Otherwise there would be no valid reason for the angel giving John the information contained in v. 18, at this point in the prophetic narrative. An interpretation that gained currency in the period following the Reformation was that 666 stood for Vicarius Filii Dei, meaning "vicar of the Son of God," one of the titles for the pope of Rome. The numerical value of the component letters of this title totals 666. (Nichol, *The Seventh-day Adventist Bible Commentary*, Volume 7) (ANF The Ante-Nicene Fathers, edited by Alexander Roberts and James Donaldson)

Modern translations remove the identity of the beast power as well as its mark by changing keywording thus changing the very meaning of the verse itself. In the case of Revelation 15:2 NIV, the word '*mark*' has simply been removed. Victory over the beast power is not possible without victory over every aspect of his domain.

John 20:23

John 20:23, KJV:
"Whose soever sins ye **remit**, they are **remitted** unto them; and whose soever sins ye **retain**, they are **retained**."

John 20:23, NIV:
"If you **forgive** anyone's sins, their sins are **forgiven**; if you do not **forgive** them, they are not **forgiven**."

John 20:23, NKJV:
"If you **forgive** the sins of any, they are **forgiven** them; if you **retain** the sins of any, they are **retained**."

The KJV uses the archaic meaning of the words remit and remitted. The English Oxford Dictionary defines them this way: to refer (a matter for decision) to a higher authority—an item referred to another for consideration. It is obvious that the words 'retain' and 'retained' are not synonyms for 'forgive' and 'forgiven.' Mark 2:7 and 1 John 1:9 makes it very plain that God only can forgive sins.

> "Whosoever sins ye remit," said Christ, "they are remitted; ... and whosoever sins ye retain, they are retained." Christ here gives no liberty for any man to pass judgment upon others. In the Sermon on the Mount He forbade this. It is the prerogative of God. But on the church in its organized capacity He places a responsibility for the individual members. Toward those who fall into sin, the church has a duty, to warn, to instruct, and if possible to restore. "Reprove, rebuke, exhort," the Lord says, "with all long-suffering and doctrine." 2 Timothy 4:2. Deal faithfully with wrongdoing. Warn every soul that is in danger. Leave none to deceive themselves. Call sin by its right name. Declare what God has said in regard to lying, Sabbathbreaking, stealing, idolatry, and every other evil. "They which do such things shall not inherit the kingdom of God." Galatians 5:21. If they persist in sin, the judgment you have declared from God's word is pronounced upon them in heaven. In choosing to sin, they disown Christ; the church must show that she does not sanction their deeds, or she herself dishonors her Lord. She must say about sin what God says about it. She must deal with it as God directs, and her action is ratified in heaven. He who despises the authority of the church despises the authority of Christ Himself. (White, *Desire of Ages*, p. 805)
>
> Christ gave no ecclesiastical right to forgive sin, nor to sell indulgences, that men may sin without incurring the displeasure of God, nor did he give his servants liberty to accept a gift or bribe for cloaking sin, that it may escape merited censure. Jesus charged his disciples to preach the remission of sin in his name among all nations; but they themselves were not

empowered to remove one stain of sin from the children of Adam. Nor were they to execute judgment against the guilty; the wrath of an offended God was to be proclaimed against the sinner; but the power which the Roman Church assumes to visit that wrath upon the offender is not established by any direction of Christ; he himself will execute the sentence pronounced against the impenitent. Whoever would attract the people to himself as one in whom is invested power to forgive sins, incurs the wrath of God, for he turns souls away from the heavenly Pardoner to a weak and erring mortal. (White, *The Spirit of Prophecy*, Vol. 3, p. 245)

"Why doth this man thus speak blasphemies? Who can forgive sins but God only?" (Mark 2:7, KJV).

Ephesians 6:12

Ephesians 6:12, KJV:
"For we wrestle not against flesh and blood, but against principalities, against powers, against the rulers of the darkness of this world, against **spiritual wickedness in high places.**"

Ephesians 6:12, NIV:
"For our struggle is not against flesh and blood, but against the rulers, against the authorities, against the powers of this dark world and against the **spiritual forces of evil in the heavenly realms.**"

Ephesians 6:12, NKJV:
"For we do not wrestle against flesh and blood, but against principalities, against powers, against the rulers of the darkness of this age, against **spiritual hosts of wickedness in the heavenly places.**"

Obviously, there is no spiritual forces or hosts of wickedness and evil in heavenly places since Lucifer was expelled from there. The spiritual wickedness in high places mentioned in the KJV refers to the league of devils and evil men in authority in this world as the following so aptly articulates in Selected Messages volume three:

> Christ shows that without the controlling power of the Spirit of God humanity is a terrible power for evil. Unbelief, hatred of reproof, will stir up satanic influences. Principalities and powers, the rulers of the darkness of this world, and spiritual wickedness in high places, will unite in a desperate companionship. They will be leagued against God in the person of His saints. By misrepresentation and falsehood they will demoralize both men and women who to all appearances believe the truth. False witnesses will not be wanting in this terrible work. (White, *Selected Messages*, Book 3, p. 416)

So why then are there verses in the modern Bible versions that say otherwise? Could these modern versions be telling us a vastly different gospel, a gospel more Gnostic beneath the surface? The following verse concluding this chapter on the mark of the beast is the most blasphemous yet. Which begs the question, are modern versions trying to convince us that Lucifer is Christ?

Revelation 13:1

Revelation 13:1, KJV:
"And **I stood upon the sand of the sea**, and saw a beast rise up out of the sea, having seven heads and ten horns, and upon his horns ten crowns, and upon his heads the name of blasphemy."

Revelation 13:1, NIV:
"**The dragon stood on the shore of the sea**. And I saw a beast coming out of the sea. It had ten horns and seven heads, with ten crowns on its horns, and on each head a blasphemous name."

At first glance, it does not seem to make sense to interject the dragon as standing on the seashore. However, considering Revelation 10: 1–2 we see that it is Jesus Christ, described in verse 1, who is standing with one foot on the sea and the other on the earth—symbolizing His dominion over all things. It is Satan, the usurper who interjects himself in place of Christ as the all-powerful one, as so blasphemously stated in the NIV and, in some fashion, most all the other modern versions. The God's Word version actually says, "the serpent stood on the sandy shore of the sea."

> The mighty angel who instructed John was no less a personage than Jesus Christ. Setting His right foot on the sea, and His left upon the dry land, shows the part which He is acting in the closing scenes of the great controversy with Satan. This position denotes His supreme power and authority over the whole earth. The controversy had waxed stronger and more determined from age to age, and will continue to do so, to the concluding scenes when the masterly working of the powers of darkness shall reach their height. Satan, united with evil men, will deceive the whole world and the churches who receive not the love of the truth. But the mighty angel demands attention. He cries with a loud voice. He is to show the power and authority of His voice to those who have united with Satan to oppose the truth. (White, *Bible Commentary*, Vol. 7, p. 971)

CHAPTER 8

The New (age) King James Versions

"Then the king commanded to call the magicians, and the astrologers, and the sorcerers, and the Chaldeans, for to shew the king his dreams. So they came and stood before the king" (Dan. 2:2, KJV).

Ellen G. White, the most prolific female author of the nineteenth century, penned the book, *The Great Controversy*. Next to the Bible, it is the most important book you will ever read. She had this to say about modern spiritualism:

> It is true that spiritualism is now changing its form and, veiling some of its more objectionable features, is assuming a Christian guise. But its utterances from the platform and the press have been before the public for many years, and in these its real character stands revealed. These teachings cannot be denied or hidden.

Even in its present form, so far from being more worthy of toleration than formerly, it is really a more dangerous, because a more subtle, deception. **While it formerly denounced Christ and the Bible, it now professes to accept both.** But the Bible is interpreted in a manner that is pleasing to the unrenewed heart, while its solemn and vital truths are made of no effect. Love is dwelt upon as the chief attribute of God, but it is degraded to a weak sentimentalism, making little distinction between good and evil. God's justice, His denunciations of sin, the requirements of His holy law, are all kept out of sight. The people are taught to regard the Decalogue as a dead letter. **Pleasing, bewitching fables captivate the senses and lead men to reject the Bible as the foundation of their faith.** Christ is as verily denied as before; but Satan has so blinded the eyes of the people that the deception is not discerned.

There are few who have any just conception of the deceptive power of spiritualism and the danger of coming under its influence. Many tamper with it merely to gratify their curiosity. They have no real faith in it and would be filled with horror at the thought of yielding themselves to the spirits' control. But they venture upon the forbidden ground, and the mighty destroyer exercises his power upon them against their will. Let them once be induced to submit their minds to his direction, and he holds them captive. It is impossible, in their own strength, to break away from the bewitching, alluring spell. Nothing but the power of God, granted in answer to the earnest prayer of faith, can deliver these ensnared souls.

All who indulge sinful traits of character, or willfully cherish a known sin, are inviting the temptations of Satan. They separate themselves from God and from the watchcare of His angels; as the evil one presents his deceptions, they are without defense and fall an easy prey. Those who thus place themselves in his power little realize where their course will end. Having achieved their overthrow, the tempter will employ them as his agents to lure others to ruin. (White, *The Great Controversy*, p. 557–558; emphasis added)

The New King James Version, as well as all the other modern versions, provides a vehicle for the legitimacy of the present form of spiritualism mentioned by Ellen White in the above quote.

The NKJV omits the words "Lord" sixty-six times, "God" fifty-one times, "heaven" fifty times, "repent" forty-four times, "blood" twenty-three times, and "hell" twenty-two times. "JEHOVAH" is entirely omitted, "new testament" entirely, "damnation" entirely, and "devils" is omitted entirely. It ignores the KJV Greek Textus Receptus over 1,200 times.

If the KJV contained these words, doesn't it makes sense, if those words are omitted, that we could be looking at a counterfeit Bible? Matthew 4:4 says: "But he answered and said, It is written, Man shall not live by bread alone, but by every word that proceedeth out of the mouth of God." The question for the NKJV authors is how

> *One of the sure signs of spiritualism is the belief that the dead are not really dead.*

are we to live by all the words of God when so many of them have been omitted? "All scripture is given by inspiration of God …" "For the prophecy came not in old time by the will of man: but holy men of God spake as they were moved by the Holy Ghost" (2 Tim. 3:16, 2 Peter 1:21, KJV).

Spiritualism

One of the sure signs of spiritualism is the belief that the dead are not really dead. Whether the belief is that the dead inhabits or haunts a house or building, they are gone up to heaven or down to hell, or they are in limbo or purgatory—it's all spiritualism or at least one aspect of spiritualism.

The New King James Version is a promoter of spiritualism in subtle, and sometimes in not so subtle ways. We will explore a few of them:

In the following verses "hell" has been replaced in the NKJV and most modern Bible versions with the transliterated Greek word "Hades" and the Hebrew word "Sheol": Matthew 11:23; 16:18, Luke 10:15; 16:23, Acts 2:27, 31, Revelation 1:18; 6:8; 20:13, 14, 2 Samuel 22:6, Job 11:8; 26:6, Psalm 16:10; 18:5; 86:13; 116:3, Isaiah 5:14; 14:15; 57:9, and Jonah 2:2.

According to Strong's Hebrew and Greek Dictionaries, the word "hell" in Jonah 2:2 was translated from the Hebrew word "Sheol" (H7585)—"the world of the dead (as if a subterranean retreat), including its accessories and inmates: —grave, hell, pit.". It shares a common definition with the Greek word "hades" (G86)—"the place (state) of departed souls: —grave, hell." Many of the King James Bible translators had a functional command of the Greek and Hebrew languages, thus they translated the words "hades" and "sheol" as "pit," "grave," and "hell" because those words better communicated the intent of the Scriptures in the English language. The words "hades" and "sheol" have pagan and spiritualistic overtones, something God specifically forbade. The English word "hell"' had no such connotation in the Bible until theologians intertwined pagan beliefs with Christianity.

"In Greek mythology, Hades the god of the underworld was a son of the Titans Cronus and Rhea. He had three sisters, Demeter, Hestia, and Hera, as well as two brothers, Zeus, the youngest of the three, and Poseidon" (http://1ref.us/nt, accessed June 26, 2018).

> [These] unfamiliar Greek and Hebrew words (says Max Kline, the author of *What's New In The New King James Version? The New Protestant Bible or a Subtle Counterfeit?* pages 30–31) [are designed to] confuse the laity and cause them to lose interest in the Bible or to seek answers from the self appointed Hebrew/Greek scholars (your local leaders), most of whom couldn't say one simple sentence in either language. These "seminary graduates," who know how to pronounce some Hebrew and Greek

words, have convinced many they have special loftiness, and the option of condescending when their "wisdom" is needed ... Is this what God intended? We could take a wild shot in the dark and say that God provided an English Bible for us so we wouldn't have to learn Hebrew and Greek ..."

The NKJV removes the word "hell" twenty-three times, replacing it with "Hades" and "Sheol!" Webster's New Collegiate Dictionary defines Hades as: "the underground abode of the dead in Greek mythology." The Bible now includes spiritualistic and mythological elements. Hades is not always a place of torment or terror! The Assyrian Hades is an abode of blessedness with silver skies called "Happy Fields." In the satanic New Age Movement, Hades is an intermediate state of purification.

The Aquarian Conspiracy, written by the late occultist Marilyn Ferguson, features on its cover a symbol known in the occult world as a Mobius. It was also known as a Triquetra in the ancient mythological religions. The symbol looks a lot like the one on the cover of the NKJV.

This symbol was removed from its cover for a time when it caused some to look on the NKJV unfavorably. It has since resurfaced on the newer editions. It must not have generated enough opposition to unfavorably affect sales. It is said occultists mark what belongs to them by hiding their symbols in plain sight.

The triquetra symbol predates Christianity. It began as the Celtic's symbol of a triune moon goddess. She was associated with the lunar phases—when the moon was waxing, waning, and full. The triquetra was also a symbol of the god Odin. Also, considered to represent the triplicates of mind, body, and soul, as well as the three domains of the world—earth, sea, and sky according to Celtic legend. In Wiccan and Neopagan belief, the triquetra symbolizes the triple aspected goddess (maid, mother, and crone). Some Christians have protested these associations of the symbol. However, even the Christian fish symbol was derived from an early symbol of Venus, represented by the female generative organs.

> The term New Age refers to the coming astrological Age of Aquarius. The New Age aims to create "a spirituality without borders or confining dogmas" that is inclusive and pluralistic. It holds to "a holistic worldview," emphasizing that the Mind, Body, and Spirit are interrelated and that there is a form of monism and unity throughout the universe. It attempts to create "a worldview that includes both science and spirituality" and embraces a number of forms of mainstream science as well as other forms of science that are considered fringe.
>
> Western spiritual and metaphysical traditions are infused with influences from self-help and motivational psychology, holistic health, parapsychology, consciousness research and quantum physics".
>
> The New Age movement includes elements of older spiritual and religious traditions like Monotheism, Pandeism, Pantheism, and Polytheism combined with Science and Gaia philosophy; particularly Archaeoastronomy, Astronomy, Ecology, Environmentalism, the Gaia hypothesis, UFO religions, Psychology, and Physics.
>
> New Age practices and philosophies sometimes draw inspiration from major world religions: Buddhism, Taoism, Chinese folk religion, Christianity, Hinduism, Sufism, Judaism (especially Kabbalah), Sikhism; with strong influences from East Asian religions, Esotericism, Gnosticism, Hermeticism, Idealism, Neopaganism, New Thought, Spiritualism, Theosophy, Universalism, and Wisdom tradition. (Based on Wikipedia, http://1ref.us/np, accessed June 26, 2018)

Don't let the term "new age" fool you; it is nothing but the repackaging of the same old spiritualism. It borrows elements from all the old spiritual and apostate religious traditions listed here.

In his denunciation of astrology and other forms of spiritualism, Daniel made this statement in Daniel 2:27: "The secret which the king hath demanded cannot the wise men, the astrologers, the magicians, the soothsayers, shew unto the king."

In the book of Hebrews, chapter 9 verse 26, is an example of how the NKJV incorporates the New Age agenda in their version of the Bible. Notice how the NKJV renders the word 'age' the same as the NIV does. Although the NKJV authors insist they followed the KJV translators and only removed the archaic words, this is one of many examples where they followed the other modern versions rendering of that word.

Hebrews 9:26, KJV:
"For then must he often have suffered since the foundation of the world: but now once in the end of the **world** hath he appeared to put away sin by the sacrifice of himself."

Hebrews 9:26, NIV:
"Otherwise Christ would have had to suffer many times since the creation of the world. But he has appeared once for all at the culmination of the **ages** to do away with sin by the sacrifice of himself."

> *Don't let the term "new age" fool you; it is nothing but the repackaging of the same old spiritualism.*

Hebrews 9:26, NKJV:
"He then would have had to suffer often since the foundation of the world; but now, once at the end of the **ages**, He has appeared to put away sin by the sacrifice of Himself."

You may say, so what, what's the big deal? Well, let's examine how the choice of the word "ages" alters the meaning of Scripture, leading the reader to believe in a dispensational model.

> Dispensationalism is a religious interpretive system for the Bible. It considers Biblical history as divided deliberately by God into defined periods or ages to each of which God has allotted distinctive administrative principles. According to

dispensationalist interpretation, each age of the plan of God is thus administered in a certain way, and humanity is held responsible as a steward during that time. (http://1ref.us/nq, accessed June 26, 2018)

In 1 John 4:14, the Father sent the Son to be the Savior of the world. However, according to New Age philosophy, "a god, one of many, sends a son, or avatar, with a message, to be a Savior, for each age." Another example of the NKJV following the lead of the other modern versions as opposed to faithfully sticking to the KJV translators as they claimed they had done is found in Luke 20:35. Jesus is explaining to the Sadducees, who didn't believe in a resurrection, that in heaven or the new earth there is no marriage like there is here on earth.

Luke 20:35, KJV:
"But they which shall be accounted worthy to obtain that **world**, and the resurrection from the dead, neither marry, nor are given in marriage."

Luke 20:35, NIV:
"But those who are considered worthy of taking part in the **age** to come and in the resurrection from the dead will neither marry nor be given in marriage."

Luke 20:35, NKJV:
"But those who are counted worthy to attain that **age**, and the resurrection from the dead, neither marry nor are given in marriage."

The word '*world*' denotes a literal place, not a mere allotment of time as the word '*age*' suggests. Note the significance of this change:

> Those who in the judgment are "accounted worthy" will have a part in the resurrection of the just. Jesus said: "They which shall be accounted worthy to obtain that world, and the resurrection

from the dead, ... are equal unto the angels; and are the children of God, being the children of the resurrection." Luke 20:35, 36. (White, *The Great Controversy*, p. 482)

The KJV and the Spirit of Prophecy are clearly in agreement here: the use of the word '*world*' signifies a literal place and not merely an allotment of time as the word '*age*' suggests. Here are more verses where the NKJV takes the position of most of the other modern versions and replace '*world*' with '*age*': Matthew 13:39–40; Matthew 28:20; Mark 10:30; Luke 20:34; Galatians 1:4; Ephesians 1:21; Ephesians 3:9, and Hebrews 9:26.

Ecumenism

Ecumenism is another form of New Age occultism. "Ecumenism refers to efforts by Christians of different church traditions to develop closer relationships and better understandings. The term is also often used to refer to efforts towards the visible and organic unity of different Christian churches in some form" (http://1ref.us/nr, accessed June 26, 2018).

The COEXIST movement, according to Wikipedia, is an ecumenical organization founded in London, United Kingdom, in 2006 by Tarek Elgawhary. The COEXIST Foundation is based in Washington, D.C., and London, U.K. it aims to advance social cohesion, and its stated mission is to promote, encourage and support engagement between Jews, Christians, and Muslims through dialogue, education, and research.

The lettering in the word **COEXIST** is designed to emphasize the representation of all the various religions, including the pagan religions. The letter 'c,' made to look like a crescent moon with star, represents Islam. The letter 'o' representing what we have come to know as the universal peace symbol, was first used in the occult religions as an upside down broken cross, representing the rejection of Jesus Christ. The 'e' represents gender inclusiveness. The letter 'x' symbolized by what is thought to be the star of David representing Judaism, is actually a hexagram in the occult religions. The letter 'i' dotted with a circled pentagram represents the pagan witchcraft religions. The 's' makes the yin and yang symbol for the eastern religions. This symbol represents the cohesiveness of good and evil, the one cannot exist without the other. And last is the letter 't' symbolized by a cross with a halo around it. Many Christians believe this to be a symbol of Christianity when it is actually a symbol for sun worship in pagan religions and apostate Christianity.

It appears to many, if not most evangelicals that ecumenism is only a movement to unite Christian religions on what they have in common. Nothing could be further from the truth. If you watch closely you will see that the Vatican is attempting to bring all religion under her control, Christian and non-Christian alike. Ecumenism more aptly fits the New Age's coexist movement. Amos 3:3 justifiably asks: "Can two walk together, except they be agreed?"

Genesis 3:5

According to New Age philosophy, finite man is or can obtain equality with the infinite God, the Creator of all things. That is why I believe the NKJV rendering of Genesis 3:5 was changed from the KJV translation "ye shall be as gods" to the critical text of the modern versions "you will be like God." More than likely Eve would never have fallen for Satan's deception had he tried to make her believe she would be like the creator God.

Genesis 3:5, KJV:
"For God doth know that in the day ye eat thereof, then your eyes shall be opened, and **ye shall be as gods**, knowing good and evil."

Genesis 3:5, NIV:
"For God knows that when you eat of it your eyes will be opened, and **you will be like God**, knowing good and evil."

Genesis 3:5, NKJV:

"For God knows that in the day you eat of it your eyes will be opened, and **you will be like God**, knowing good and evil."

Mankind was created in the likeness of God from the very beginning, according to Genesis 1:26 and Genesis 5:1. The term "ye shall be as gods" implies autonomous gods. In fact, that was the actual temptation.

> In the councils of heaven God said, "Let us make man in our image, after our likeness.... So God created man in his own image, in the image of God created he him" (Genesis 1:26, 27). The Lord created man's moral faculties and his physical powers. All was a sinless transcript of Himself. God endowed man with holy attributes, and placed him in a garden made expressly for him. Sin alone could ruin the beings created by the hand of the Almighty.—*The Youth's Instructor*, July 20, 1899. (White, *Selected Messages*, Book 3, p. 133)

Adam and Eve were already like God, just as you and I are created in the image of God. And although you and I are like God, we are not God, as the term "ye shall be as gods" implies.

Romans 1:25

Romans 1:25, KJV:

"Who **changed** the **truth of God into a lie**, and worshipped and served the creature more than the Creator, who is blessed for ever. Amen."

Romans 1:25, NIV:

"They **exchanged** the **truth about God for a lie**, and worshiped and served created things rather than the Creator—who is forever praised. Amen."

Romans 1:25, NKJV:
"Who **exchanged** the **truth of God for the lie**, and worshiped and served the creature rather than the Creator, who is blessed forever. Amen."

The NKJV, like the other modern versions, turns the Word of God into a lie every time they substitute words that alter the meaning of scripture. Notice both the NIV and the NKJV substitute the words "into a" with the words "for the." Subtle as this change may appear to the casual reader, those with spiritual discernment can see that the KJV speaks of those who deliberately twist the meaning of scripture. Genesis 3:4 is one of the clearest examples in the Bible of how the changing, in this case adding a word to Scripture, *"changed the truth of God into a lie"* as opposed to *"exchanged the truth of God for the lie."*

For many Christian faiths, the Scriptures mean to them something that they do not say. For example, many of them believe that the dead are not dead, they are alive either in purgatory, limbo, hell, hades, sheol, or heaven. Though Scripture says differently, they believe the opposite of what Scripture actually does say. This is what is meant by "**changing** the truth **into** a lie." To "**Exchange** the truth **for the** lie" means to replace the truth for something other than the truth. The phrase, "for the lie," gives the connotation of some specific lie with no clarification of what that lie is. No one deliberately exchanges the truth for a lie.

> To all students we would say, In the name of the Lord do not permit yourselves to be held where the spiritual atmosphere is poisoned with skepticism and falsehood. Those who have had the evidence of truth, but who for days, weeks, months, and years have had about them a subtle influence that gives a distorted representation, a false coloring, to the truth of God, are not fit for teachers for our youth. Where falsehoods regarding the word and work of God are reported as truth is no place for students who are preparing for the future, immortal life. We

are seeking heaven, wherein can enter none who have **changed the truth of God into a lie**. (White, *Manuscript Releases*, Vol. 12, p. 125; emphasis added)

In the days of Christ … Men had well-nigh ceased to discern God in His works. The sinfulness of humanity had cast a pall over the fair face of creation; and instead of manifesting God, His works became a barrier that concealed Him. Men "worshiped and served the creature more than the Creator." Thus the heathen "became vain in their imaginations, and their foolish heart was darkened." Romans 1:25, 21. So in Israel, man's teaching had been put in the place of God's. Not only the things of nature, but the sacrificial service and the **Scriptures themselves**—all given to reveal God—were so perverted that they became the means of concealing Him. (White, *Christ's Object Lessons*, p. 18: emphasis added)

Thus, it is today with the advent of modern Bible versions.

Acts 17:22

On the surface, the subtle differences between the words '*superstitious*' and '*religious*' may not be readily apparent. However, these words are different in meaning and therefore render a different meaning of the verses itself.

Act 17:22, KJV:
"Then Paul stood in the midst of Mars' hill, and said, *Ye* men of Athens, I perceive that in all things ye are too **superstitious**."

Act 17:22, NIV:
"Paul then stood up in the meeting of the Areopagus and said: "People of Athens! I see that in every way you are **very religious**."

Act 17:22, NKJV:

"Then Paul stood in the midst of the Areopagus and said, "Men of Athens, I perceive that in all things you are **very religious**."

Superstition is an excessively credulous belief in and reverence for supernatural beings or a widely held but unjustified belief in supernatural causation leading to certain consequences of an action or event, or practice based on such a belief. Whereas *religion* is the belief in and worship of a superhuman controlling power, especially a personal God or gods, a particular system of faith and worship. While religion can contain elements of superstition, the two terms are not synonymous.

Ares and Cupid are mythological Greek gods. Ares who supposedly murdered the Greek god Poseidon's son Halirrhothius was tried by the gods for his crime at the Areopagus. The Areopagus is located northwest of the Acropolis in Athens, Greece. Its English name is the composite form of the Greek name Areios Pagos, translated "Ares Rock." In ancient times, it functioned as the court for trying murder cases.

As you can see, superstition was the backbone of the ancient Greek's religion. It influenced Pagan as well as Papal Roman religion.

> In that hour of solemn responsibility, the apostle was calm and self-possessed. His heart was burdened with an important message, and the words that fell from his lips convinced his hearers that he was no idle babbler. "Ye men of Athens," he said, "I perceive that in all things ye are too superstitious. For as I passed by, and beheld your devotions, I found an altar with this inscription, To the Unknown God. Whom therefore ye ignorantly worship, Him declare I unto you." With all their intelligence and general knowledge, they were ignorant of the God who created the universe. Yet there were some who were longing for greater light. They were reaching out toward the Infinite. (White, *The Acts of the Apostles*, p. 237)

The NKJV and other modern versions attempt to put religion and superstition at the same level, it can be easily seen by defining the two words, that replacing the word "superstition" with "religion" changes the meaning of the verse entirely.

Superstition is spiritualism. When one's religion contains elements of superstition that religion is also spiritualism. So, if one is truly Christian, why not simply call religion, religion and superstition, superstition. This is a perfect example of changing the truth into a lie. The working of Satan, through spiritualism, has infiltrated Christianity from its very inception. And we now have modern Bible versions that support it.

Is it possible there could have been or is now a New Age agenda in mind for making these changes? The creators of the NKJV assert that their intention for creating their new version was to make it clearer and easier to read. If that was their true motivation, it seems logical that they would have continued the use of the KJV Greek text translated as *gods*, *world*, and *superstition* rather than changing them to the Critical Greek Text translations *like God*, *age*, and *religion*. Those so-called improvements only created confusion—and we all know who the author of confusion is.

CHAPTER 9

Ellen White's Use of Modern Bible Versions

"At the mouth of two witnesses, or at the mouth of three witnesses, shall the matter be established" (Deut. 19:15, KJV).

There are many in our ranks who take the viewpoint that Ellen White presented no inspiration on modern Bible versions and made no statements warning against the use of them. Thus, they conclude that the absence of a denunciation from her constitutes an endorsement. They further argue that the usages of other Bible versions appearing in her writings are another clear indication of her endorsement of them. Also, references from the following statements made by Willie C. White in 1931 and later published in April 1947, are used as circumstantial evidence of an endorsement by her:

> I do not know of anything in the E. G. White writings, nor can I remember of anything in Sister White's conversations, that

would intimate that she felt that there was any evil in the use of the Revised Version. ...

When the first revision was published, I purchased a good copy and gave it to mother. She referred to it occasionally, but never used it in her preaching. Later on, as manuscripts were prepared for her new books and for revised editions of books already in print, Sister White's attention was called from time to time by myself and Sister Marian Davis, to the fact that she was using texts which were much more clearly translated in the Revised Version. Sister White studied each one carefully, and in some cases she instructed us to use the Revised Version. **In other cases she instructed us to adhere to the Authorized Version.**

When Testimonies for the Church, Volume Eight, was printed and it seemed desirable to make some lengthy quotations from the Psalms, it was pointed out to Sister White that the Revised Version of these Psalms was preferable, and that by using the form of blank verse the passages were more readable. Sister White gave the matter deliberate consideration, and instructed us to use the Revised Version. **When you study these passages you will find that in a number of places where the Revised Version is largely used, the Authorized Version is used where translation seems to be better.**

We cannot find in any of Sister White's writings, nor do I find in my memory, any condemnation of the American Revised Version of the Holy Scriptures. Sister White's reasons for not using the A.R.V. in the pulpit are as follows:

"There are many persons in the congregation who remember the words of the texts we might use as they are presented in the authorized version, and to read from the revised version would introduce perplexing questions in their minds as to why the wording of the text had been changed by the revisers and as to why it was being used by the speaker." **She did not advise me in a positive way not to use the A.R.V., but she intimated to me**

quite clearly that it would be better not to do so, as the use of the different wording brought perplexity to the older members of the congregation. (E.G. White Document File 579; "Mrs. White and Revised Versions," by Arthur White, *Ministry*, April 1947, pp. 17–18)

It is clear from the above statements by Willie White that Ellen White regarded the Authorized King James Bible as the standard and advised other versions not be used when they would cause confusions. It is also clear, at least to this author, that a comparison of the King James Bible text to that of the modern versions was not made before arriving at the conclusion that Ellen White's occasional use of the RV and the ARV is, in reality, an endorsement of them. It should be painfully obvious by now as texts from modern versions are compared to the King James Version and how the Spirit of Prophecy agrees with the King James that the Holy Spirit could not possibly be endorsing the modern versions. The council provided by the Holy Spirit through the vehicle of Ellen White is another witness to the authenticity of the King James Version Bible as well as the authenticity of the inspiration of Ellen White.

Ellen White, James White, and other pioneers of this movement have either made reference to or actually quoted from the Apocrypha books. Do any of us really believe they were endorsing these books that at best contain conjecture and at worse outright spiritualism? Before I understood how evil it was to be entertained by sin, I used to go to the movies and watch television. I even, to this day, quote some of the "good" dialogs from those movies. I hope and pray that anyone who has ever heard me verbalize such a quote did not go away believing that I was endorsing that movie in any way, shape, or form.

Divine Preservation

Some have misconstrued the following statement from *Early Writings* to mean that there are mistakes in the Authorized King James Bible because well-meaning men changed the word of God in an attempt to make it more understandable. And that God has accepted those changes and His Word is still clear in spite of them. Let us take a closer look at this quote:

> I saw that God had especially guarded the Bible; yet when copies of it were few, learned men had in some instances changed the words, thinking that they were making it more plain, when in reality they were mystifying that which was plain, by causing it to lean to their established views, which were governed by tradition. But I saw that the Word of God, as a whole, is a perfect chain, one portion linking into and explaining another. True seekers for truth need not err; for not only is the Word of God plain and simple in declaring the way of life, but the Holy Spirit is given as a guide in understanding the way to life therein revealed. (White, *Early Writings*, p. 220)

When copies of the Bible were few would have been in the times before the invention of the printing press, before the King James Bible existed. In the 4th century both the Codex Vaticanus, 'B' and the Codex Sinaiticus (Aleph) were supposedly produced. Some scholars believe there is evidence that points to these codices as modern nineteenth-century forgeries. However, if they are in fact authentic, then they fit in perfectly with the inspiration given to Mrs. White in the above statement. "Learned men had in some instances changed the words, thinking that they were making it plainer, when in reality they were mystifying that which was plain, by causing it to lean to their established views, which were governed by tradition."

If these two codices existed at the time the Authorized King James Bible was compiled, as some assert they did, they most certainly were not and would not have been included, as the minority manuscripts of equal unreliability were not.

A Perfect Chain

"The word of God, as a whole, is a perfect chain, one portion linking into and explaining another" (White, *Early Writings*, p. 220). The perfect chain she speaks of is clearly seen in those words that link one scripture with another. For example, the words '*seed*' and '*bruise,*' notice how the NIV breaks that perfect chain of prophecy by substituting those words:

Genesis 3:15, KJV:
"And I will put enmity between thee and the woman, and between thy **seed** and her **seed**; **it** shall **bruise** thy head, and thou shalt **bruise** his heel."

Genesis 3:15, NIV:
"And I will put enmity between you and the woman, and between your **offspring** and hers; **he** will **crush** your head, and you will **strike** his heel."

Romans 16:20, KJV:
"And the God of peace shall **bruise** Satan under your feet shortly. The grace of our Lord Jesus Christ be with you. Amen."

Romans 16:20, NIV:
"The God of peace will soon **crush** Satan under your feet. The grace of our Lord Jesus be with you."

Revelation 12:17, KJV:
"And the dragon was wroth with the woman, and went to make war with the **remnant of her seed**, which keep the **commandments of God**, and **have the testimony** of Jesus Christ."

Revelation 12:17, NIV:
"Then the dragon was enraged at the woman and went off to wage war against the rest of **her offspring**—those who keep **God's commands** and **hold fast their testimony** about Jesus."

The Hebrew word "shuph" was translated once in Genesis 3:15 of the NIV as "crush" and later in the same verse as "strike." Undoubtedly, the NIV translators know something about the connotation of English words. To say that Satan "crushed" the heel of Christ in this verse would suggest an incurable wound to the foot of Christ as the "crushing" of Satan's head does. The connotation of the word "bruise," as used by the KJV translators, gives us the understanding that in the controversy between Christ and Satan, Christ would not be unscathed. However, Satan would receive the worst of that encounter. That happened at the cross. The KJV reiterates that prophecy in Romans 16:20—Christ would "bruise" Satan again shortly, this time under the feet of His church. The remnant of her seed is the same seed (church) that bruises the head of Satan in Genesis 3:16 dislodged again by the NIV and the other modern versions usage of the words "rest of her offspring."

The NIV, as well as most modern versions, destroys the chain of words that confirm the precision of this prophecy by changing the words that link them together.

There are many examples of this chain being broken in modern versions. But the clincher can be found in the foundational prophecy of our church—Daniel 8:14, where the day for a year principle found in Numbers 14:34 and Ezekiel 4:6 has been removed from this verse in the modern versions.

Daniel 8:14, KJV:

"And he said unto me, Unto two thousand and three hundred **days**; then shall the sanctuary be **cleansed**."

Daniel 8:14, NIV:

"He said to me, 'It will take 2,300 **evenings and mornings**; then the sanctuary will be **reconsecrated**.'"

The substitution of the word *days* with the words *evenings and mornings* remove this verse from the perfect chain of prophecy the word *days* connect it to. The words *cleansed* and *reconsecrated* obviously do not have the same meaning. To consecrate something is to make it holy. Why would God ever need to make the heavenly sanctuary holy again? It needs cleansing because of our sins, but if it was not holy, it could not be in heaven.

Vindication of the AV and the Prophet

Contrary to popular belief Sister Ellen White did have inspiration from God that the Word of God would be directly attacked by Satan. Let us take a look at this statement she made in *The Great Controversy*:

> It had been Rome's policy, under a profession of reverence for the Bible, to keep it locked up in an unknown tongue and hidden away from the people. Under her rule the witnesses prophesied "clothed in sackcloth." But another power—the beast from the bottomless pit—was to arise to make open, avowed war upon the word of God. (White, *The Great Controversy*, p. 269)

This other power came on the scene in the late 18th century in the form of secular humanism, atheism, and/or scientific reasoning during and after the French Revolution. The sinner-friendly New Age Bibles are the results of the reemergence of the Romish power. It still wars against the word of God, but in its original subtle, covert way. Now in the form of counterfeit Bibles.

Dr. Benjamin G. Wilkinson, in defense of his book *Our Authorized Bible Vindicated*, in a June 1930 General Conference committee meeting where he was accused of authoring a book without their permission that undermined the work of the church, stated the following:

> In the Index to the writings of Mrs. E G White, I find that in 28 volumes of her works that are listed that she is credited with

making 15,117 references to the Bible. Of these more than 95 out of every 100 are from the AV (KJV), and therefore less than 5 in 100 are from the Revised Version and all other versions combined. Less than 14 are from the Noyes', Leesers', and Rotherhams's Versions. The RV was issued in 1881, and more than three fourths of the works of Sister White, listed in the Index were published after that date, so that the RV was accessible while more than three-fourths of her books were being written. In one of her books she gives 406 references to the AV (KJV) and 65 to other versions. This is the largest departure from the AV in any of her works. In another she gives 940 references to the AV, to 59 in the RV and ARV. In Volume 8 of the Testimonies she quotes the AV 666 times, the ARV 53 times, and the RV 3 times. In this volume she refers 45 times to the O.T., in the ARV, only 8 times to the New Testament. She quotes the poetical Psalms sometimes entire and other Old Testament scriptures where the change is largely verbal and slight. In another large book she makes 865 quotations from the AV and 4 from the Revised Version. In several she makes only one quotation from the RV to several hundred in the AV. With this mathematically exact evidence before you, no one can truthfully say that she showed any preference for the Revised Version, or by any means regarded it as on an equality with the AV, but the very opposite. It is a most significant fact that she made no reference whatever, so far as the Index indicates, quoted not one verse in the Revised Version in Volume 9 of the "Testimonies," the last Testimony of the Spirit of Prophecy to the Church. This is also true of 13 other books listed in the index, nearly all of them written after the Revised Version was published, the prophet of the Lord began with the AV alone; she closed with the AV alone. It was to her evidently the supreme authority. (Wilkinson, B.G., *Answers to Objections*, Section 4, p. 9)

In his book, *The Dismantling of Seventh-day Adventism*, H.H. Meyers discusses Wilkinson and Ellen White's use of the King James (or Authorized) Version:

> Wilkinson also reminded the Committee of Sister White's historical statements which endorsed the Textus Receptus of Erasmus which included correction of errors in the Vulgate, thus giving us a Bible that had clearer sense; giving new impetus to the work of reform (the Reformation); and completing, through Tyndale, the giving of the Bible to England. (see *The Great Controversy*, p. 245).
>
> By using the RV sparingly Sister White used only those texts which she considered put the same meaning as the AV plainer, and that she used numerous texts from the AV that were considered by the revisers of the AV Committee to be spurious. Therefore she was not endorsing the trustworthiness of the RV as a whole, but rather subordinated all but a few texts to the King James Version.
>
> It is pertinent to note that at this time Dr. Wilkinson was probably unaware of Willie White's statement about other people instigating his mother's use of the revised versions as recorded in *Problems in Translation*. This book was not published until the year 1954 *(See* Chapter Five). Nor does he give any evidence of awareness of certain of the leaders' propensities to fiddle with her writings.
>
> According to [Dr Gilbert M.] Valentine [*The Shaping of Adventism*], who bases his information on a letter written by A.O. Tait, editor of the "Signs", to W A Spicer (November 25, 1929), it seems that revised versions had been inserted in some of her writings without permission. According to Tait, he had personally heard G.B. Starr tell of an alleged conversation with

> Sister White on the matter of her use of the Revised Version. She is recorded as saying that *she would like to know who was responsible for the Revised Versions being used in her later writings*. And again, *she had never given authority for anything of that sort* (*The Shaping of Adventism*, p. 270). (Meyers, *The Dismantling of Adventism*, p. 22–23)

"The church in the wilderness," and not the proud hierarchy enthroned in the world's great capital, was the true church of Christ, the guardian of the treasures which God has committed to His people to be given to the world (White, *The Great Controversy*, p. 64).

> A little reflection on this statement should make it abundantly clear that Sister White knew nothing by the year 1888 (in which "The Great Controversy" was published) of the scheming subterfuge orchestrated by Rome that resulted in the Revised Version. If we cannot assume so, then great doubts must be placed on her intelligence and probity, for our examination of historical documentation shows that the Revised Version really is a child of that illegitimate union of church and state, *enthroned in the world's great capital*.
>
> Further, we can see God's guidance in preventing her from using the Revised Version in preaching, and in her endorsement of the King James Version as God's divine standard, by which she cautiously compared all other versions. Our humanity may lead us to wonder why God did not reveal Rome's subterfuge to His messenger, especially in view of the fact that detractors of the Spirit of Prophecy usually take great delight in upholding Sister White's use of the Revised Version as bestowing divine sanction. This hypocritical anomaly should set alarm bells ringing.

In considering such a proposition it is well to observe that practically all who love to deprecate Sister White's role as God's messenger and prophet are lovers of modern versions.

Having noted this fact and its implications, it is well to reflect on the role of prophets throughout the ages. Can we name even one to whom God saw fit to reveal everything? If so, one prophet alone would have been sufficient to reveal His will to man.

Who, for instance, among the Old Testament prophets, was inspired to condemn the practice of slavery? Why did Paul, that (26) great exponent of Christianity, not condemn slavery? Does this mean that slavery is acceptable in God's sight? Not at all! God has given us the power of reason which tells us that slavery is one of the worst examples of transgressing His moral law which says: *Thou shalt not steal*; for what more can there be to steal from a person who has been deprived of the freedom to regulate the use of his body and time? The very term "slavery" is the one used by God to denote total subservience to Satan and sin.

> *We cannot presume to understand all of God's purposes and ways, nor should we attempt to rationalize His dealings with men.*

Yet God impelled Sister White to speak out strongly against slavery when He considered the time opportune. We cannot presume to understand all of God's purposes and ways, nor should we attempt to rationalize His dealings with men. We must accept the fact that Mrs. White did not explicitly speak out against the use of modern versions, but God did lead her to adopt a cautious approach to them while absolutely retaining the Bible of the Reformation as the standard of truth. Speaking of the Bible with which she was familiar, she explains: *The Scriptures were given to men, not in a continuous chain of unbroken utterances, but piece by piece through successive generations, as God in His providence saw a fitting opportunity to impress man at sundry times and divers places* ("1 Selected Messages", pp. 19, 20). (Meyers, *The Dismantling of Adventism*, p. 13–14)

2 Peter 1:21

God has been pleased to communicate His truth to the world by human agencies, and He Himself, by His Holy Spirit, qualified men and enabled them to do this work. **He guided the mind in the selection of what to speak and what to write**. The treasure was entrusted to earthen vessels, yet it is, nonetheless, from Heaven. The testimony is conveyed through the imperfect expression of human language, yet it is the testimony of God; and the obedient, believing child of God beholds in it the glory of a divine power, full of grace and truth. (White, *My Life Today*, p. 41; emphasis added)

2 Peter 1:21, KJV:
"For the prophecy came not in old time by the will of man: **but holy men of God** spake as they were **moved** by the Holy Ghost."

2 Peter 1:21, NIV 2011:
"For prophecy never had its origin in the human will, **but prophets**, though human, spoke from God as they were **carried along** by the Holy Spirit."

2 Peter 1:21, NIV 1984:
"For prophecy never had its origin in the will of man, **but men** spoke from God as they were **carried along** by the Holy Spirit."

2 Peter 1:21, NIrV 2014:

"It never came simply because a prophet wanted it to. Instead, the Holy Spirit guided the prophets as they spoke. So, although prophets are human, prophecy comes from God."

God did not select just anyone to speak for Him when He wanted to deliver a prophetic message to His people. The King James Bible says he selected holy men, men who sought to serve God in the way He required. The very prerequisite of a prophet is that he or she live a holy life. When they cease from a holy life, they become false prophets. The implications of *carried along*, an idiom, could mean to persuade someone or to carry physically or to transport them. The connotation for *moved*, in this case, is, to stir the emotions or arouse to action. These words are not interchangeable as the modern interpreters would have you to believe. The 2011 NIV upgrades mere *men* in the 1984 edition to *prophet* status. Perhaps they were mistaken in 1984. Are we to believe the source documents for these renderings changed over those few years or shall we apply the more obvious observation which is, they are changed at the whim of men, and not holy men?

> *God did not select just anyone to speak for Him when He wanted to deliver a prophetic message to His people.*

Many Seventh-day Adventist insists that the RV and the ARV get their legitimacy from Ellen G. White's use of them. They even go as far as projecting that claim on the more modern versions like the NIV, NKJV, NASB, etc.; when these Bibles did not exist during her lifetime. As you have seen throughout this book so far, modern versions are in fact opposed to the plain writings of Mrs. White.

I do not know why the Lord did not give Mrs. White direct light on the dangers of modern versions. Perhaps, had the church taken the 1888 messages seriously, this issue would have been nonexistent. What I do know is that by her using the legitimate verses in these modern versions, credibility by default is given to those illegitimate verses that are at variance with her writings.

Many of the same verses in the NIV and the NKJV that conflict with the KJV cited in this book can also be found in the RV and the ARV. Those verses from the RV and the ARV were not referenced because those versions are not as popular, nor do they sell as much, as the NIV and the NKJV. Any good counterfeit must incorporate as much as possible what is considered authentic characteristics of the original. Otherwise, they will not deceive anyone. The NKJV, NIV, RV, ARV, etc. are good counterfeits, but they do have flaws that identify them as counterfeits. A sampling of those flaws is exposed in this book. The fact that Ellen White never used those bogus verses, which were considered by her as bad translations, should be telling. To him who has a discerning ear, let him hear.

CHAPTER 10

The Destruction of the Sanctuary

> "And let them make me a sanctuary; that I may dwell among them" (Exod. 25:8, KJV).

As a people, we should be earnest students of prophecy; we should not rest until we become intelligent in regard to the subject of the sanctuary, which is brought out in the visions of Daniel and John. This subject sheds great light on our present position and work, and gives us unmistakable proof that God has led us in our past experience. **It explains our disappointment in 1844**, showing us that **the sanctuary to be cleansed** was not the earth, as we had supposed, but that Christ then entered into the most holy apartment of the heavenly sanctuary, and is there performing the closing work of His priestly office, in fulfillment of the words of the angel to the prophet Daniel**, "Unto two thousand and three hundred days; then shall the sanctuary be cleansed."**

Our faith in reference to the messages of the first, second, and third angels was correct. The great way-marks we have passed are immovable. Although the hosts of hell may try to tear them from their foundation, and triumph in the thought that they have succeeded, yet they do not succeed. **These pillars of truth stand firm as the eternal hills, unmoved by all the efforts of men combined with those of Satan and his host.** We can learn much, and should be constantly searching the Scriptures to see if these things are so. **God's people are now to have their eyes fixed on the heavenly sanctuary, where the final ministration of our great High Priest in the work of the judgment is going forward,—where He is interceding for His people.** (White, "Notes of Travel: The Maine Camp-Meeting," *Review and Herald*, November 27, 1883; emphasis added)

The sanctuary services are a microcosm of the plan of salvation in whom Jesus Christ is the central figure. Asaph, a Levite, a prophet, one of King David's chief musicians, choir leader, and author of Psalms 50 and 73 through 83 "was envious at the foolish, when [he] saw the prosperity of the wicked." He said in Psalm 73:17 that it wasn't until he went into the sanctuary of God; that he understood the fate of the wicked. After observing the sanctuary services, Asaph saw and understood the plan of salvation. He understood how God is dealing with the sin problem. This is one of the main reasons Psalm 77:13 (below) is distorted in most of the modern versions. It is one of the most important texts in the Bible.

> *The sanctuary services are a microcosm of the plan of salvation in whom Jesus Christ is the central figure.*

Psalm 77:13, KJV:
"Thy way, O God, **is in the sanctuary**: who is so great a God as our God?"

Psalm 77:13, NIV:
"Your ways, O God, **are holy**. What god is as great as our God?"

As stated many times earlier, the NIV is representative of like distortions in all modern versions. The KJV shows that God's "way is in the sanctuary." In other words, His mode of operating is demonstrated in the sanctuary services. Of course, God's "way" is holy as the NIV says, but what does that tell us about how He operates? It is understood from Genesis, the first book in the Bible, that God's way is holy, but the importance of the sanctuary is made clearer to us in this verse. The testimony of Jesus makes it even clearer in the verses below demonstrating the existence of the sanctuary in heaven:

Exodus 15:17, KJV:
"Thou shalt bring them in, and plant them in the mountain of thine inheritance, in the place, O LORD, which thou hast made for thee to dwell in, **in the Sanctuary, O Lord, which thy hands have established.**"

Psalm 102:19, KJV:
"For he hath looked down **from the height of his sanctuary**; from heaven did **the LORD behold the earth.**"

Hebrews 8:1–2, KJV:
"Now of the things which we have spoken this is the sum: We have such an high priest, who is set on the right hand of the throne of the Majesty in the heavens; **A minister of the sanctuary, and of the true tabernacle, which the Lord pitched, and not man.**"

Hebrews 8:5, KJV:
"Who serve unto the example and shadow of heavenly things, as Moses was admonished of God when he was about to make the tabernacle: for, See, saith he, that thou make all things **according to the pattern shewed to thee in the mount.**"

Revelation 11:19, KJV:
"And **the temple of God was opened in heaven**, and there was seen in his temple the ark of his testament: and there were lightnings, and voices, and thunderings, and an earthquake, and great hail."

Revelation 15:5, KJV:
"And after that I looked, and, behold, **the temple of the tabernacle of the testimony in heaven** was opened."

Daniel 8:14

The prophecy of Daniel 8:14 is crucial to the understanding of the heavenly sanctuary because it makes an application that directly connects the typical earthly sanctuary service to the antitypical sanctuary service taking place in heaven. This connection is broken in the modern versions:

Daniel 8:14, KJV:
"And he said unto me, Unto two thousand and three hundred **days**; then shall the sanctuary be **cleansed**."

Daniel 8:14, NIV:
"He said to me, 'It will take 2,300 **evenings and mornings**; then the sanctuary will be **reconsecrated**.'"

"The scripture which above all others had been both the foundation and the central pillar of the advent faith was the declaration: 'Unto two thousand and three hundred days; then shall the sanctuary be cleansed.' Daniel 8:14" (White, *The Great Controversy*, 1911, p. 409).

The use of the word *reconsecrated* by the NIV interpreters means to rededicate to a holy use. The use of this word is the direct result of the use of "dynamic equivalence" discussed earlier. Besides, according to Ecclesiastes 3:14, Solomon said: "I know that, whatsoever God doeth, it shall be for ever: nothing can be put to it, nor any thing taken from it: and

God doeth it, that men should fear before him." Therefore the heavenly sanctuary would never need to be re-consecrated. However, it does need cleansing from the sins placed there.

Daniel 8:14 is a reference to the heavenly sanctuary contrary to modern scholarship's attempt to make it the earthly. The earthly sanctuary had already been destroyed at the writing of the book of Daniel. The reference to 2,300 years into the future also suggests this as the heavenly sanctuary. The use of the words *"evenings and mornings"* as opposed to *"days"* attempts to weaken the day for a year prophetic principle found in Numbers 14:34 and Ezekiel 4:6 that applies to this verse.

When identical words are changed in one text that links them to other text that uses that same word, the chain of evidence is broken, and the proof of a doctrine is weakened as a result.

Daniel 9:24–27

Daniel 9:24–27, KJV:

> **Seventy weeks** are determined upon thy people and upon thy holy city, to finish the transgression, and to make an end of sins, and to make reconciliation for iniquity, and to bring in everlasting righteousness, and to seal up the vision and prophecy, and to anoint the **most Holy**. Know therefore and understand, that from the going forth of the commandment to restore and to build Jerusalem unto the Messiah the Prince shall be **seven weeks, and threescore and two weeks**: the street shall be built again, and the wall, even in troublous times. And **after threescore and two weeks** shall Messiah be cut off, **but not for himself**: and the people of the prince that shall come shall destroy the city and the sanctuary; and the end thereof shall be with a flood, and unto the end of the war desolations are determined. And he shall confirm the covenant with many for **one week**: and in the midst of the **week** he shall cause the sacrifice and the

oblation to cease, **and for the overspreading of abominations he shall make it desolate, even until the consummation, and that determined shall be poured upon the desolate.**

Daniel 9:24–27, NIV:

Seventy 'sevens' are decreed for your people and your holy city to finish transgression, to put an end to sin, to atone for wickedness, to bring in everlasting righteousness, to seal up vision and prophecy and to anoint the **Most Holy Place**. "Know and understand this: From the time the word goes out to restore and rebuild Jerusalem until the Anointed One, the ruler, comes, there will be **seven 'sevens,' and sixty-two 'sevens.'** It will be rebuilt with streets and a trench, but in times of trouble. After the **sixty-two 'sevens,'** the Anointed One will be put to death **and will have nothing**. The people of the ruler who will come will destroy the city and the sanctuary. The end will come like a flood: War will continue until the end, and desolations have been decreed. He will confirm a covenant with many for **one 'seven.'** In the middle of the **'seven'** he will put an end to sacrifice and offering. **And at the temple he will set up an abomination that causes desolation, until the end that is decreed is poured out on him.**

The seventy weeks in Daniel 9:24 is a time prophecy pointing to a probationary or grace period extended to the Jewish nation by God. They were to: 1) finish the transgression, 2) make an end of sin, 3) make reconciliation for iniquity, 4) bring in everlasting righteousness, 5) seal up the vision and prophecy, and 6) anoint the most holy.

This probationary period of seventy weeks was in reality 490 years when the day for a year principle from Numbers 14:34 and Ezekiel 4:6 are applied to a prophetic day. Seventy weeks determined or cut off from the 2,300-day prophecy of Daniel 8:14 are equal to 490 days (70 × 7 = 490).

Most people understand that seven days make up a week and can, therefore, connect the word "week" to "days." However, connecting the words "seventy sevens" to "days" is a bit of a stretch, unless of course, one brings their King James Version understanding to the reading of the NIV.

The words *'anoint the most Holy'* are correctly interpreted in verse 24 of the KJV. Not *'Most Holy Place'* as it appears in all the modern versions interpretation from the Nestles/Aland Critical Greek text. This verse is a prophecy of the anointing of the Messiah, Jesus Christ, not the holiest apartment of the sanctuary, that anointing or dedication was done when it was completed in 408 B.C. See Ezra 6:15–17.

Daniel 9:25 of the KJV gives further evidence that Jesus Christ is to be anointed and not the *'Most Holy Place,'* as stated in the NIV. It says that 'Messiah the Prince will come on the scene at the end of 69 prophetic weeks or 483 (69 × 7 = 483) literal years after the decree to restore and rebuild Jerusalem. You would never be able to understand this prophecy nor ascertain 69 weeks from the NIV's 'seven sevens and sixty-two sevens' without first understanding the King James Bible.

The decree to restore and rebuild Jerusalem was given by King Artaxerxes of Persia in 457 BC, see Ezra 6:14 and 7:11–26. Four hundred and eighty-three years later, AD 27, Christ was anointed (–457 BC + 483 = AD 26). Because there is no such thing as year zero, as indicated on a number line, a year must be added to AD 26 bring us to AD 27.

Verse 26 is a restating of verse 25 but adds additional information to the prophecy which includes the Messiah's death. However, in this verse, the prophecy begins at the completion of the seven prophetic weeks or 49 literal years. The additional threescore and two prophetic weeks, or 434 literal years equal a total of 483 literal years when Messiah the Prince/Jesus Christ was anointed at His baptism.

When Jesus was cut off or crucified, it was not for Himself as the KJV rightly states. He was cut off for us. He died for our sins. What does "... and will have nothing" (NIV) mean anyway? When Christ died on the cross, He causes the sacrifice and oblation to cease in verse 27. Yet the same Christ that causes the sacrifices to cease sets up an abomination that causes desolation until the end that is decreed by Him (Christ) is poured out on Himself, according to the NIV. This is nonsense of the highest order.

Here is how the Testimony of Jesus, also known as the Spirit of Prophecy agrees with the King James Bible, proving that the spirits of the prophets are subject to the prophets (1 Corinthians 14:32, KJV):

> The burden of Christ's preaching was, "The time is fulfilled, and the kingdom of God is at hand; repent ye, and believe the gospel." Thus the gospel message, as given by the Saviour Himself, was based on the prophecies. The "time" which He declared to be fulfilled was the period made known by the angel Gabriel to Daniel. "Seventy weeks," said the angel, "are determined upon thy people and upon thy holy city, to finish the transgression, and to make an end of sins, and to make reconciliation for iniquity, and to bring in everlasting righteousness, and to seal up the vision and prophecy, and to anoint the most holy." Daniel 9:24. A day in prophecy stands for a year. See Numbers 14:34; Ezekiel 4:6. The seventy weeks, or four hundred and ninety days, represent four hundred and ninety years. A starting point for this period is given: "Know therefore and understand, that from the going forth of the commandment to restore and to build Jerusalem unto the Messiah the Prince shall be seven weeks, and threescore and two weeks," sixty-nine weeks, or four hundred and eighty-three years. Daniel 9:25. The commandment to restore and build Jerusalem, as completed by the decree of Artaxerxes Longimanus (see Ezra 6:14; 7:1, 9, margin), went into effect in the autumn of B. C. 457. From this time four hundred and eighty-three years extend to the autumn of A. D. 27. According to the prophecy, this period was to reach to the Messiah, the Anointed One.

> In A. D. 27, Jesus at His baptism received the anointing of the Holy Spirit, and soon afterward began His ministry. Then the message was proclaimed. "The time is fulfilled." (White, *Desire of Ages*, p. 233)

Diligent Bible prophecy students know and understand that Daniel 9:24–27 is a time prophecy pointing to the very year that Jesus Christ would be anointed and take up His public three-and-one-half-year ministry at the end of the sixty-ninth week, AD 27. It points to His being cut off or crucified in the midst of the seventieth week, verse 26. It shows the crucifixion as the event that ended the sacrificial system and the consummation of the Abrahamic covenant. It not only reveals the conditions of the Jewish probation but both the starting point of the construction of Jerusalem and the Temple over a 490-year period in verses 24 and 25. It even predicts the very destruction of Jerusalem and the earthly sanctuary in AD 70, verse 27. The decimated wording of this very important prophecy in the modern versions can only be termed as nothing short of diabolical.

Exodus 30:6 and Hebrews 10:20

Exodus 30:6, KJV:
"And thou shalt put it before the **vail** that is by the ark of the testimony, before the **mercy seat** that is over the testimony, where I will meet with thee."

Exodus 30:6, NIV:
"Put the altar in front of the **curtain** that shields the ark of the covenant law—before the **atonement cover** that is over the tablets of the covenant law—where I will meet with you."

Although a curtain and a veil can serve the same function, they are not the same thing. The use of the word veil in the KJV denotes more than a cloth for the mere separation of compartments but also the concealment of what is contained in that compartment. When the word curtain is used by the NIV translators, it denotes separation only, breaking its link with 2 Corinthians 3:13–16.

The NIV also removes the *"mercy seat"* entirely (27 times) and replaces it in most case with *"atonement cover."* (Exod. 25:17–22, 26:34, 31:7, 35:12, 37:6–9, 39:35, 40:20, Lev. 6:2, 13–15, Num. 7:89, 1 Chron. 28:11) The Spirit of Prophecy knows nothing of an "atonement cover":

> To this people were committed the oracles of God. They were hedged about by the precepts of His law, the everlasting principles of truth, justice, and purity. Obedience to these principles was to be their protection, for it would save them from destroying themselves by sinful practices. And as the tower in the vineyard, God placed in the midst of the land His holy temple.
>
> Christ was their instructor. As He had been with them in the wilderness, so He was still to be their teacher and guide. In the tabernacle and the temple His glory dwelt in the holy shekinah **above the mercy seat**. In their behalf He constantly manifested the riches of His love and patience. (White, *Christ's Object Lessons*, p. 287–288)

Hebrews 10:20, KJV:

"By a new and living way, which he hath consecrated for us, through the **veil**, that is to say, his flesh."

Hebrews 10:20, NIV:

"By a new and living way opened for us through the **curtain**, that is, his body."

The NIV's replacement of the linking word *veil* with *curtain* breaks the chain that links the veil that separates the Holy from the Most Holy Place as a symbol of Christ—"By a new and living way, which he hath consecrated for us, through the *veil*, that is to say, his flesh" (Hebrews 10:20 KJV).

Curtains surrounded the entire outer court of the tabernacle, and to use the word *curtain* in the place of *veil* diminishes Christ's role as Savior. Christ is the antitype of the typical veil that separated the Holy Place from the throne of God—the mercy seat.

> "After he had offered one sacrifice for sins forever," he "sat down on the right hand of God; from henceforth expecting till his enemies be made his footstool. For by one offering he hath perfected forever them that are sanctified.... Having therefore, brethren, boldness to enter into the holiest by the blood of Jesus, by a new and living way, which he hath consecrated for us, through the veil, that is to say, his flesh; and having an high priest over the house of God; let us draw near with a true heart in full assurance of faith, having our hearts sprinkled from an evil conscience, and our bodies washed with pure water.... And let us consider one another to provoke unto love and to good works." ("The Worth of Souls," *Review and Herald*, March 17, 1903, par. 4)

Hebrews 7:21 and 10:21

Hebrews 7:21, KJV:
"(For those priests were made without an oath; but this with an oath by him that said unto him, The Lord sware and will not repent, **Thou art a priest for ever after the order of Melchisedec:**)"

Hebrews 7:21, NIV:
"But he became a priest with an oath when God said to him: 'The Lord has sworn and will not change his mind: "**You are a priest forever.**"'"

By removing the words *"after the order of Melchisedec,"* the precedence for Christ as the high priest has been taken away. In the typical earthly sanctuary service, only Levites could serve as priests. Jesus was not a Levite and could not possibly be a high priest of the Levitical order. He would have had to be a priest of another order—the order of Melchisedec. The purpose of the sanctuary serving as an object lesson—or a microcosm—of the plan of salvation is especially destroyed in this verse by the modern versions. The earthly sanctuary services being typical has been effectively detached from the antitypical heavenly sanctuary service.

Hebrews 10:21, KJV:
"And having an **high priest** over the house of God."

Hebrews 10:21, NIV:
"And since we have a **great priest** over the house of God."

The ancient or typical sanctuary services, as stated above, demonstrate how we are saved. To unlink the chain of similar word uses as the NIV does, removes Christ as *high priest* with the use of the words *great priest*. The high priest of the typical service can be found in Exodus 28 and Leviticus 21.

Leviticus 16:16 and Hebrews 9:12

Leviticus 16:16, KJV:
"And he shall make an atonement for the **holy place**, because of the uncleanness of the children of Israel, and because of their transgressions in all their sins: **and so shall he do for the tabernacle of the congregation**, that remaineth among them in the midst of their uncleanness."

Leviticus 16:16, NIV:
"In this way he will make atonement for the **Most Holy Place** because of the uncleanness and rebellion of the Israelites, whatever their sins have been. **He is to do the same for the Tent of Meeting**, which is among them in the midst of their uncleanness."

A careful study of the words "tabernacle of the congregation" and the "holy place" reveal that they are in fact the same place (see Exodus 30:22–38, KJV). The holy place is symbolic of where Jesus, our high priest, intercedes on behalf of His people in the typical sanctuary services. In Isaiah 14:13 of the KJV, we see that is the place where Satan intends to exalt his rulership. "For thou hast said in thine heart, I will ascend into heaven, I will exalt my throne above the stars of God: I will sit also upon the mount of the congregation, in the sides of the north." This connection between verses cannot be made in the modern versions because of the changes in the wordings of the verses.

In nearly all the modern versions the verses in Leviticus 16 (verses 16, 20, 23, 27, and 33) were changed from "holy place" to "Most Holy Place." For these changes to be correct, the entire order of the sanctuary service would have to be changed also. However, to support the change in the order of the antitypical service in Hebrews 9:12 of the modern versions, the linking text in Leviticus required changing also. The statement below represents the actual order of the typical service in Leviticus 16:16:

> Such was the work that went on, day by day, throughout the year. The sins of Israel were thus transferred to the sanctuary, and a special work became necessary for their removal. God commanded that an atonement be made for each of the sacred apartments. "He shall make an atonement for the holy place, because of the uncleanness of the children of Israel, and because of their transgressions in all their sins; and so shall he do for the tabernacle of the congregation, that remaineth among them in the midst of their uncleanness." [Leviticus 16:16, 19.] An atonement was also to be made for the altar, to "cleanse it, and hallow it from the uncleanness of the children of Israel." [Leviticus 16:16, 19.] (White, *The Great Controversy* 1888, p. 418)

Hebrews 9:12, KJV:
"Neither by the blood of goats and calves, but by his own blood he entered in once into the **holy place**, having obtained eternal redemption for us."

Hebrews 9:12, NIV:
"He did not enter by means of the blood of goats and calves; but he entered the **Most Holy Place** once for all by his own blood, having obtained eternal redemption."

Hebrews 9:12, NKJV:
"Not with the blood of goats and calves, but with His own blood He entered the **Most Holy Place** once for all, having obtained eternal redemption."

Jesus' sacrifice for us on the cross, where He obtained eternal redemption for us, cannot mean that He entered the most holy place in the heavenly sanctuary. Christ's ministry in the heavenly sanctuary follows the pattern given to us in the earthly sanctuary service. The lamb that was slain in the outer court (the earth) represented what Jesus would do by dying on the cross. His mediatorial work is performed daily in the holy place, and His judgment work is performed in the most holy place once a year in the typical earthly service, on the day of atonement. The context of Hebrews 9 follows this pattern.

The Cross and Its Shadow by Stephen N. Haskell is an excellent book on this subject that includes enough biblical references for a sound theological position on this subject.

In Exodus 26:33 the NIV translates the same Hebrew word *Qodesh* as both the "holy place" and the "most holy place." Yet did not make the same distinction with the Greek word *hagion* in Hebrews 9:12 when the context of the verse makes it clear that it is the holy place spoken of and not the most holy place.

> For eighteen centuries this work of ministration continued in the first apartment of the sanctuary. The blood of Christ,

pleaded in behalf of penitent believers, secured their pardon and acceptance with the Father, yet their sins still remained upon the books of record. As in the typical service there was a work of atonement at the close of the year, so before Christ's work for the redemption of men is completed, there is a work of atonement for the removal of sin from the sanctuary. This is the service which began when the 2300 days ended. At that time, as foretold by Daniel the prophet, our High Priest entered the most holy, to perform the last division of his solemn work,—to cleanse the sanctuary. (White, *The Great Controversy* 1888, p. 421)

The sanctuary service and its connection to Jesus Christ and the plan of salvation are difficult enough to teach from the King James Bible—which totally supports this doctrine. It is near, if not entirely impossible, to explain by using the modern versions. This alone should be enough to make any serious Christine stay far from these spurious Bibles.

CHAPTER 11

The Conclusion of the Matter

"Fear God, and give glory to him; for the hour of his judgment is come: and worship him that made heaven, and earth, and the sea, and the fountains of waters" (Rev. 14:7, KJV).

It is interesting how the Spirit of Prophecy connects the famine for the Word of God, Amos chapter 8, to the end of the world:

> As Jesus moved out of the most holy place, I heard the tinkling of the bells upon His garment; and as He left, a cloud of darkness covered the inhabitants of the earth. There was then no mediator between guilty man and an offended God. While Jesus had been standing between God and guilty man, a restraint was upon the people; but when He stepped out from between man and the Father, the restraint was removed and Satan had entire control of the finally impenitent. It was impossible for the plagues to be poured out while Jesus officiated in

the sanctuary; but as His work there is finished, and His intercession closes, there is nothing to stay the wrath of God, and it breaks with fury upon the shelterless head of the guilty sinner, who has slighted salvation and hated reproof. In that fearful time, after the close of Jesus' mediation, the saints were living in the sight of a holy God without an intercessor. Every case was decided, every jewel numbered. Jesus tarried a moment in the outer apartment of the heavenly sanctuary, and the sins which had been confessed while He was in the most holy place were placed upon Satan, the originator of sin, who must suffer their punishment.

Then I saw Jesus lay off His priestly attire and clothe Himself with His most kingly robes. Upon His head were many crowns, a crown within a crown. Surrounded by the angelic host, He left heaven. The plagues were falling upon the inhabitants of the earth. Some were denouncing God and cursing Him. Others rushed to the people of God and begged to be taught how they might escape His judgments. But the saints had nothing for them. The last tear for sinners had been shed, the last agonizing prayer offered, the last burden borne, the last warning given. The sweet voice of mercy was no more to invite them. When the saints, and all heaven, were interested for their salvation, they had no interest for themselves. Life and death had been set before them. Many desired life, but made no effort to obtain it. They did not choose life, and now there was no atoning blood to cleanse the guilty, no compassionate Saviour to plead for them, and cry, "Spare, spare the sinner a little longer." All heaven had united with Jesus, as they heard the fearful words, "It is done. It is finished." The plan of salvation had been accomplished, but few had chosen to accept it. And as mercy's sweet voice died away, fear and horror seized the wicked. With terrible distinctness they heard the words, "Too late! too late!"

Those who had not prized God's Word were hurrying to and fro, wandering from sea to sea, and from the north to the east, to seek the Word of the Lord. Said the angel, "They shall not find it. There is a famine in the land; not a famine of bread, nor a thirst for water, but for hearing the words of the Lord. What would they not give for one word of approval from God! but no, they must hunger and thirst on. Day after day have they slighted salvation, prizing earthly riches and earthly pleasure higher than any heavenly treasure or inducement. They have rejected Jesus and despised His saints. The filthy must remain filthy forever." (White, *Early Writings*, p. 280–281; emphasis added)

The pure words of the Lord are to be treasured above all earthly treasure. In this day of a multiplicity of modern Bible versions, it seems but few cherish the Word of God. The average professor of Christianity has no idea how the Bible came to us. They have a blind trust that what their pastors tell them is the truth. They have no experiential knowledge of the Word. When modern versions are introduced, they blindly trust them also. Is there any wonder that even now there is a famine for hearing the Word of God?

> *The pure words of the Lord are to be treasured above all earthly treasure.*

The prophet Amos prophesied and the modern-day prophetess, Ellen G. White, echoes that a famine for God's Word would take place in the last days of this earth's history. As men reject the plain teachings of God's word for the spurious renditions of modern Bible versions, the true words of God are systematically replaced with the inventions of cunning and crafty men. We are admonished in the following quote that the time would come when a thorough knowledge and understanding of God's word would be imperative:

> "Search the Scriptures; for in them ye think ye have eternal life." Every position of truth taken by our people will bear the criticism of the greatest minds; the highest of the world's great men will be brought in contact with truth, and therefore every position we take should be critically examined and tested by the Scriptures. Now we seem to be unnoticed, but this will not always be. Movements are at work to bring us to the front, and if our theories of truth can be picked to pieces by historians or the world's greatest men, it will be done. (White, *Evangelism*, p. 69)

The Seventh-day Adventist movement is a prophetic movement in fulfillment of the third angel's message of Bible prophecy, Revelation 14:12; and as the above quote says, "Every position of truth taken by our people will bear the criticism of the greatest minds..."

> There is no religious enterprise going forward in the land except this by the Seventh-day Adventists, which claims to be a fulfilment of the third angel's message,—no other which holds forth, as its prominent themes, the very subjects of which this message is composed. What shall we do with these things? Is this the fulfilment?—It must so stand, unless its claims can be disproved: unless it can be shown that the first and second messages have not been heard: that the positions taken in reference to the beast, image, mark, and worship are not correct; and that all the prophecies, and signs, and evidences which show that the coming of Christ is near, and consequently that this message is due, can be wholly set aside. But this the intelligent

Bible student will hardly undertake." (Smith, *Daniel and the Revelation*, p. 670)

The Majority Text and the Textus Receptus, used to compile the King James Version (KJV), are the Bible resources used by the pioneers of the Protestant Reformation. All its doctrines and beliefs were fashioned with them. As modern Bible versions became more abundant in society and in the churches, no doubt they were a contributing factor to the changes in Protestant beliefs and practices becoming a widespread phenomenon. The first of the modern English translation Bible versions were of the New Testament in 1881, called the Revised Version (RV) or the English Revised Version (ERV). The Old Testament of the RV was released in 1885. It is evident that all modern Bible versions that follow the tradition of the first revised Bible version differ in many ways from the Authorized Version in which the Protestant church pioneers derived its doctrine. If these modern Bible versions are to be considered God's true word and are to be used to support the doctrines that distinguish Protestants from popery, the Protestant churches would have very shaky biblical footing for its beliefs and should rightfully close their doors. There are many Protestant churches today clasping hands with Roman-ism, owing, in large part, to modern Bible versions.

This book contains a small sampling of the many changes that can be found in modern Bible versions. However, when the totality of all the changes made in modern versions are considered, and every changed scripture dissected, we see the emergence of a gospel foreign to the Protestant reformers. We see the emergence of a popish hue with the stamp of ecumenism all over it. We see the diabolical plotting of Satan conspiring with evil men to overthrow the plans of God. We see a programmed effort to undermine the true Word of God by placing it under a mountain of erroneous Bible versions casting doubt on the only exact English Bible—the King James Authorized Version.

No matter how many times the declaration is made that the Authorized King James Version of the Bible is the best English Bible to date, there will be those who attempt to disprove the validity of that statement by lumping those who believe it in a category they've labeled King James Only-ism. King James Only-ists are considered a group of fanatical individuals with purely an unfounded emotional attachment to the King James Bible. They are even accused of worshiping it as an idol. No doubt, there are some with purely emotional attachments to the KJV as there are those who cling to their modern versions for the same reason. However, this accusation is usually an ad hominem attack. If the reader has not understood that the writer of this book is basing his assertions on comparing Scripture and facts, he hopes that the following reiteration clears the matter up:

Virtually all modern Bible versions come from the minority stream of manuscripts, codices, papyri scraps, etc. The use of this stream of material is dominated by the Codex Sinaiticus (Aleph) and the Vaticanus B, which are considered the oldest and best by some scholars, and mere counterfeits by others. The widely accepted Critical Greek Text, was compiled initially by German rationalist, Rudolf Kittel, Eberhard Nestle, and later Kurt Aland. It is from editions of the Critical Greek Text primarily compiled by these men, where we get the modern Bible versions. That is why they all read so much alike. The King James Bible comes from an entirely different stream of codices and manuscripts. These are called the Majority Text and Textus Receptus. The majority of the Bibles around the world, in many different languages, were compiled hundreds of years before the existence of the first modern version in 1881. These Bibles all agree with the KJV an is the reason this author prefers it.

We invite you to view the complete
selection of titles we publish at:
www.TEACHServices.com

We encourage you to write us
with your thoughts about this,
or any other book we publish at:
info@TEACHServices.com

TEACH Services' titles may be purchased in
bulk quantities for educational, fund-raising,
business, or promotional use.
bulksales@TEACHServices.com

Finally, if you are interested in seeing
your own book in print, please contact us at:
publishing@TEACHServices.com

We are happy to review your manuscript at no charge.

www.ingramcontent.com/pod-product-compliance
Lightning Source LLC
Chambersburg PA
CBHW070554160426
43199CB00014B/2495